I AM YAHWEH

I
AM
YAHWEH

Walther Zimmerli

Translated by Douglas W. Stott

Edited by and Introduction by
Walter Brueggemann

John Knox Press
ATLANTA

I Am Yahweh
"Ich bin Yahweh"
> Geschichte und Altes Testament. Beiträge zur historischen Theologie 16. Albrecht Alt zum 70. Geburtstag dargebracht, 1953, pp. 179–209. Verlag J. C. B. Mohr (Paul Siebech), Tübingen. Reprinted in Gottes Offenbarung: Gesammelte Aufsätze I, Theologische Bücherei 19 (München: Chr. Kaiser Verlag, 1969), pp. 11–40. (Permission granted.)

Knowledge of God According to the Book of Ezekiel
"Erkenntnis Gottes nach dem Buch Ezechiel"
> Eine theologische Studie. Abhandlungen zur Theologie des Alten und Neuen Testaments 27, 1954. Zwingli-Verlag, Zürich. Reprinted in Gottes Offenbarung: Gesammelte Aufsätze I, Theologische Bücherei 19 (München: Chr. Kaiser Verlag, 1969), pp. 41–119. (Permission granted.)

The Word of Divine Self-Manifestation (Proof-Saying): A Prophetic Genre
"Das Wort des göttlichen Selbsterweises (Erweiswort), eine prophetische Gattung"
> Mélanges Bibliques rédigés en l'honneur de André Robert. Travaux de l'institut catholique de Paris 4. Bloud et Gay, 1957, pp. 154–64. Reprinted in Gottes Offenbarung: Gesammelte Aufsätze I, Theologische Bücherei 19 (München: Chr. Kaiser Verlag, 1969), pp. 120–132. (Permission granted.)

Plans for Rebuilding After the Catastrophe of 587
"Planungen für den Wiederaufbau nach der Katastrophe von 587"
> Vetus Testamentum XVIII, 1968, pp. 229–55. Verlag E. J. Brill, Leiden. Reprinted in Studien zur alttestamentlichen Theologie und Prophetie: Gesammelte Aufsätze II, Theologische Bücherei 51 (München: Chr. Kaiser Verlag, 1974), pp. 165–91. (Permission granted.)

Unless otherwise indicated, Scripture verses are the author's translations. However, whatever the source the author always uses Yahweh for the LORD.

Library of Congress Cataloging in Publication Data

Zimmerli, Walther, 1907-
  I am Yahweh.

  Includes bibliographical references.
  Contents: I am Yahweh — Knowledge of God according to the book of Ezekiel — The word of divine self-manifestation (proof-saying): a prophetic genre — Plans for rebuilding after the catastrophe of 587.
  1. Bible. O.T. Ezekiel—Criticism, interpretation, etc.—Addresses, essays, lectures. 2. God—Biblical teaching—Addresses, essays, lectures. I. Stott, Douglas W. II. Title.
BS1545.2.Z5513   224'.406   81-85326
ISBN 0-8042-0519-1   AACR2

Contents

ABBREVIATIONS

ANET	Ancient Near Eastern Texts Relating to the Old Testament, ed. J. B. Pritchard
AOT², AOB²	Altorientalische Texte (Bilder) zum Alten Testament, ed. H. Greẞmann, 2nd edition (1926/7)
ATD	Das Alte Testament Deutsch. Neues Göttinger Bibelwerk
BBB	Bonner Biblische Beiträge
B Ev. Theol.	Beiträge zur Evangelischen Theologie
BHK³	Biblia Hebraica, ed. R. Kittel, tertia editio
BHT	Beiträge zur Historischen Theologie
BK	Biblischer Kommentar. Altes Testament, ed. M. Noth
BWA(N)T	Beiträge zur Wissenschaft vom Alten (und Neuen) Testament
BZAW	Beiheft zur Zeitschrift für die alttestamentliche Wissenschaft
c.t.	corrected text
Ev. Theol.	Evangelische Theologie
FRLANT (NF)	Forschungen zur Religion und Literatur des Alten und Neuen Testaments (Neue Folge)
HAT	Handbuch zum Alten Testament, ed. O. Eissfeldt
HK	Handkommentar zum Alten Testament, ed. W. Nowack
HSAT⁴	Kautzsch-Bertholet, Die Heilige Schrift des Alten Testaments, 4th ed. 1922 f.
JBL	Journal of Biblical Literature
KHK	Kurzer Hand Commentar, ed. K. Marti
LXX	Septuagint
NTD	Das Neue Testament Deutsch. Neues Göttinger Bibelwerk
OLZ	Orientalistische Literaturzeitung
OTS	Oudtestamentische Studien
RGG³	Die Religion in Geschichte und Gegenwart, 3rd ed.
SAT²	Die Schriften des Alten Testaments, 2nd ed.
ThB	Theologische Bücherei
ThLZ	Theologishe Literaturzeitung
ThR (NF)	Theologische Rundschau (Neue Folge)
ThDNT	Theological Dictionary of the New Testament
VT (Suppl)	(Supplement to) Vetus Testamentum
WMANT	Wissenschaftliche Monographien zum Alten und Neuen Testament
WO	West des Orients
ZAW	Zeitschrift für die alttestamentliche Wissenschaft
ZDMG	Zeitschrift der Deutschen Morgenländischen Gesellschaft
ZThK	Zeitschrift für Theologie und Kirche

Translator's Preface

Because of Walther Zimmerli's inclination to take up topics from previous works and treat them further in subsequent ones, and because many of his works have already been translated, a certain problem arose concerning the consistency of translation of various key words and phrases. This problem was all the more pressing because terminology figures quite prominently in three of the following essays. Whereas previous translators may have rendered *Erkenntnisaussage* as "recognition assertion," *Erkenntnisformel* as "knowledge formula," *Selbstvorstellungsformel* as "formulaic phrase of self-introduction," and *Erweiswort* as "proof-saying," I have departed somewhat from these renderings largely because of the meanings these terms acquire within the essays. Instead of the above translations, the reader will encounter here "statement of recognition," "recognition formula," and "formula of self-introduction" (or even "self-introductory formula"). Because of its fulcral position wthin both the following essays and other works by Zimmerli, I have maintained the rendering "proof-saying," though in most cases it implies something closer to "manifestation saying." In any case, when cross-referencing other works by Zimmerli the reader need not be too apprehensive, since the *field of meaning* surrounding each of these terms remains the same throughout. Indeed, I hope the sightly different renderings will loosen the context somewhat and provide the reader with a new angle of vision from which to approach the material.

Introduction

The purpose of this volume is simply to make available in one place and in English these essays of Walther Zimmerli. The first three essays constitute a corpus of classic proportion. And the fourth essay, though somewhat later and probably not as important, shows Zimmerli working out some of the implications of his earlier, fundamental argument.

Walther Zimmerli is the distinguished Professor of Old Testament at Göttingen University. He is among that most senior and distinguished group of German scholars whose work was deeply impacted by events on the continent in and around World War II and who are unashamedly theological in their perspective and intention. The work of that generation is reflected especially in *Biblischer Kommentar*, a commentary series exhibiting a passionate theological intentionality, to which Zimmerli has contributed.

Zimmerli is at the same time a critical scholar of extraordinary power and a man of deep faith and piety. It is that combination of critical power and profound faith that marks his scholarship and notably shapes the argument in these essays.

His life work has been the massive commentary in *Biblischer Kommentar* on Ezekiel, which is universally acknowledged to be a bench mark in Ezekiel study. Brevard Childs asserts: "It is certainly fair to say that he has succeeded in inaugurating a new phase in the study of the book by his numerous articles and massive commentary. . . . It is difficult to believe that critical scholarship will ever return to a pre-Zimmerli stage in evaluating the book."[1] Fortunately the first half of the commentary has now appeared in English translation.[2] The method used in that commentary represents an important advance beyond the older commentaries.

Zimmerli is of course schooled in the methods of literary dissection, but his attention to form and especially to the ongoing dynamic of the tradition has permitted him to engage in the continued exposure and updating of the text for new situations. Building on early literary critics, Zimmerli has been able to study the literature in its dynamic development and to pay primary attention to the evangelical claims of the text. His method shows the important linkage of tradition-criticism to theological sensitivity.

Old Testament scholarship is now engaged in a sharp controversy over the role of theological intentionality in relation to criticism. The discussion now revolves around the work of Childs already cited, but it is clear that Zimmerli (and his generation of scholarship in Germany) had posed that question previously. While the more recent generation (with the notable exception of Childs) is inclined to return to a critical, pretheological perspective, the gains in this area brought about by Zimmerli and others are irreversible.

As with every serious commentary, Zimmerli's had as a by-product a number of articles, prepared as preliminary to the work itself. These articles form the body of this volume. The first three essays presented here are a part of the earliest preliminary work from which his main argument stems. Dated within a brief period (1953–57), one can observe that they embody some of Zimmerli's most fundamental theological decisions concerning Ezekiel. To be sure, some of this material has now been summarized elsewhere[3] in less complete form, but such allusions are no adequate substitute for the full argument in its initial development and presentation.

The fourth essay is dated later (1968) and obviously relates to Zimmerli's work on the later chapters of Ezekiel. Therefore it is likely not to be as important nor decisive for future work as are the other three. However, it also is not discontinuous from those crucial proposals, being linked to the other essays in two important ways. First, note that at the end of his third piece Zimmerli asks the rhetorical question: "Did the exile bring about a hiatus here?" (p. 110). The issue concerns continuity and discontinuity around the savage events of 587. In part this fourth article explores that question about the exile and the resulting hiatus. Zimmerli explores

Ezekiel 40—48 to examine the continued sovereignty of Yahweh and the form it must now take, given the decisive break point. He concludes (p. 133) that Ezekiel witnesses to the "God who in any new beginning will maintain his old promise." The rhetorical question in the third paper is answered eleven years later in the fourth paper with a balance of continuity and discontinuity. What is finally clear is that in the midst of all discontinuities, it is the continuity of God's promise that can be counted on.[4]

The fourth essay is also related to the other three in a second way.[5] At the beginning (p. 111) and end (p. 133) of the fourth essay, Zimmerli speaks of the "blessing of the nadir," "the blessing of point zero." Theologically, Zimmerli understands that Israel, and especially Ezekiel, had to hear what could be heard of God's word in a moment of despair when everything seemed silenced. It is the self-disclosure of this unfettered sovereign which makes new history possible; Zimmerli makes the point after Ezekiel that precisely at the "Nullpunkt" Yahweh's sovereignty is disclosed afresh. Thus the mode of self-disclosure and the situation of Ezekiel belong precisely together. There is, for Ezekiel, no other ground of hope than this One who can assert himself in spite of the circumstance.

As I have restudied these essays, I have been impressed again with the extraordinary power that is still to be found in them. They offer a classic example of what scholarship was about in their time, but we do not present them here simply because they are interesting historical pieces. They are more than a classic point of reference. Rather, in them Zimmerli has articulated and anticipated many of the issues and the categories which still need work today. Scholars and students will refer to these essays to learn once more how to use critical tools in the service of an articulate faith. In at least the following ways the articles will continue to be important.

1. The articles are *models of method*. Zimmerli is a master at form-critical analysis. Necessarily, the articles are technical and not easy reading. But to those who will persevere, Zimmerli shows how to stay with a text, listen to it, and watch it draw other texts into its range of proclamation. He displays marvelous patience with the Scripture as he waits for it to share its point. Inevitably one will be surprised at how much can be heard and learned from a small text, if

one will have the patience and discernment to stay with it all the way to its claim.

Conversely, Zimmerli's method is to be appreciated not only for persevering with the text, but for dealing only with the text and not bringing too much else to it. Zimmerli wrote these articles when the great constructive hypotheses of Alt, Noth, and von Rad were at their peak of influence. Now those same hypotheses are under heavy and broad attack. It is somewhat surprising how little Zimmerli is dependent upon these constructs and how little his argument is damaged by that attack, although he does not escape completely. For example, Zimmerli does appeal to Alt's hypothesis on apodictic law and to von Rad's construction on Holy War. However, it is clear that his main argument does not depend on these models, but rather on the words of the texts themselves, and that is a methodological point worthy of replication.

2. Zimmerli's work is especially important for the recent discussion of *revelation*.[6] While in these articles Zimmerli is not primarily concerned with the theoretical question of revelation,[7] the issue surfaces here almost incidentally. That is, the category of revelation is not faced on *formal* grounds apart from the actual *substance* of the revelation and the identity of the One who reveals, and yet his treatment of the matter is exceedingly important, even if incidental.

While the issue of revelation may seem to be marginal to the content of these essays, their future significance is enhanced by an understanding of the problem of revelation as Old Testament scholarship has recently discussed it. The discussion turns on some fine points, but our understanding of these issues is important for appreciating the perceptive and shrewd articulation of Zimmerli.

These articles were completed at the time of the enormous success of the notion of "The Mighty Deeds of God in History." In the United States this idea was especially urged by G. Ernest Wright and in a different way by von Rad in the first volume of his great theology.[8] It is agreed that the focus of Old Testament faith was a recital of the *events* in which God acted for Israel. Thus "revelation as history"[9] became a slogan that sought to summarize this argument, and in quite philosophical form, Pannenberg made the most of that general claim.

It is not surprising that such a program was subjected to serious criticism. While Brevard Childs issued the most programmatic critique,[10] it has been James Barr who in a series of statements most severely dismissed the claim.[11] Barr urged (a) that "revelation as history" does not account for much of the Old Testament, (b) that given our Enlightenment consciousness there are serious intellectual problems for such a notion, and (c) that the problem of two histories which are different and not effectively related has not yet been solved. Thus von Rad must always deal with a "critical" history and a "kerygmatic" history.

Subsequently Barr proposed that we may usefully move from the notion of *history* to that of *story*,[12] and while that may be helpful, I do not think it is a very major gain. I suggest that, so far as Barr is concerned, the problem has not been in *eventfulness* as the locus of God's disclosure, but rather in his understanding of "history" in Enlightenment categories. After all, it is important to note that the insistence on "historicality"[13] in relation to revelation is meant to combat an existentialist tendency in Bultmann (among others) which does not appreciate the concrete activity of revelation in the world of human experience.[14]

It is striking that much of this criticism does not apply to Zimmerli. To be sure, Childs does fault him with "this bias toward the historical,"[15] and there is no doubt that Zimmerli worked in the mileau of von Rad's credo hypothesis and was not adverse to the notion of the "recital."[16] However, Zimmerli's own argument in these essays (and in his more programmatic essay) is that the self-revelation of God occurs in the speech-formulae in which God speaks, and that when God speaks, he speaks his own name. Thus revelation is identifiable and has a specific content, but the content is none other than the name of the Speaker.

To be sure, the self-disclosure of Yahweh does not happen in a vacuum. It occurs in historical context; it is linked to historical activity.[17] But revelation for Zimmerli is never simply "interpreted historical activity." The speech is neither reflective nor explanatory, but rather an event (liberating or theophanic) which is the voice of God himself. Zimmerli makes no effort to translate this happening into other terms in order to accommodate Enlightenment categories or to make explanations. As a good exegete must, he stays close to the text, insisting that revelation is the voice of none other than God, and thus the claim for revelation is very tight. The One who speaks is none other than Yahweh, and what Yahweh says in the moment of disclosure is nothing other than speech about Yahweh.

In these essays Zimmerli draws no large conclusions and proposes no overriding constructs. He stays close to the text, and in so doing he both forces us to see the claim of the text itself and escapes some of the criticism made against his contemporaries. Methodologically he has performed with remarkable firmness. He has stayed with a very disciplined form-critical method, focusing singularly on the formulae, their context, and development. Zimmerli's substantive claim is intimately tied to the form-critical insight. What is at issue is nothing other than Yahweh's self-presentation. While contextually that self-presentation by Yahweh occurs at the "Nullpoint," theologically Yahweh's self-presentation is not dependent upon or derived from any religious property or historical circumstance. Revelation is simply that, and nothing else. Happily Zimmerli does not let this crisp reality get tangled with other claims or categories. In the light of that integrity, it seems to me that the fine distinctions about "history" and "word" are excessive and neither contribute to nor distract from the main theological gain made here.

3. And that leads to our final point: that Zimmerli's arguments are important not only for their form critical methodology and the formal claims about revelation, but for the *theological substance* discerned in the text. The form-critical method leads to exceedingly important theological affirmations. While there is no doubt that his perspective is shaped by a "theology of the Word" most commonly linked to the program of Karl Barth, Zimmerli's argument and conclusions are drawn from the text and not from preconceived notions. His conclusion, confirmed from many directions, is simply that there is an intimate, unique, and irreversible connection between the One who reveals and that which is revealed. The

revealed One is the revealing One. Yahweh has no other disclosure to make other than his own person, and his person in its hiddenness is disclosed only as he chooses to disclose it.

In making this argument on exegetical and form-critical grounds, Zimmerli shows us how to do biblical *theology*. He does not linger over comparative questions nor over issues of religious phenomenology. Rather the end result is an understanding and discernment of God that is appropriate to Yahweh and distinctive to Israel. It is that premise for faith that endures and remains constant even during the exile with which Ezekiel is preoccupied.

(a) The God revealed is an *actor* in historical experience, and if "historical" is a stumbling block, it is enough to say that God participates in a "narrative drama." The revelation is never in a vacuum, but always in a context of decisive impingement. Not incidentally then, the key formulae are found especially in the Exodus narrative. Where the name is uttered in this formulae, something is changed, and the utterance of the formula in the very mouth of God is part of that intervention.

(b) The God revealed is a *speaker*. God utters his voice and the world is reshaped and recharacterized. The speech of Yahweh is decisively revelatory, even if it is always linked to the act.

(c) This God is *inscrutably sovereign*. In these formulae, Yahweh is sovereign; that is what the disclosure is all about. The revelation is concerned with the announcement of that sovereignty, but that sovereignty is not flat, one-dimensional, or unchanging. That is why the speech is characteristically given in theophany, a speech enmeshed in awesome mystery. The announcement does not simply communicate information, but also brings the listening world to obedient, if reluctant, acknowledgement.

(d) This sovereignty is known always as *judgment and salvation*. Yahweh's self-disclosure is not a matter of casual interest, but a matter of life and death. While the formulae always have the character of liberating good news, they are at the same time always polemical against other gods.

The theological gift of these essays is enormous in that they contain the impulse for a great deal of constructive work yet to come. We may comment on two of these tasks. First, Zimmerli should be credited with discerning that the category of *promise* is foundational for the faith of Israel, and that promise is not simply a casual notion that God will do something good in the future. It is rather an affirmation of the resilient faithfulness of God. This idea became crucial precisely in the exile when all other sources of hope were gone, and it is especially in exilic literature (P, Ezekiel, and Second Isaiah) that these formulae appear with such extraordinary force.

It is not easy to assess the influence of Zimmerli on current theologies of hope. Meeks[18] scarcely mentions Zimmerli, while giving much more credit to von Rad. That may indeed be correct, but we should note two factors. First, it is with Zimmerli's notion of word/history that Rendtorff and Pannenberg carry on much of their conversation. Second, in his own work[19] Zimmerli has been preoccupied with hope and gave particular attention to Ernst Bloch who has so much influenced Moltmann. I suspect that there is more to Zimmerli's contribution in this area than has yet been recognized.

Second, much more work is yet to be done on the proclamation of the name. Both Zimmerli[20] and von Rad[21] have seen the decisive importance of the second commandment which prohibits images. The juxtaposition of the *announcement* of Yahweh at the beginning of the decalogue and the immediate *polemic* against other gods is structurally important to the faith of Israel.[22] Everything is at stake in the announcement of the Name, in its being heard and honored properly. For where the name is not announced, or not heard, where Yahweh is not presented, the chance for distortion and faithlessness is enormous.

I suggest that Genesis 2—3 is indicative of what happens when the name is not disclosed. In Genesis 2:4b–24 and 3:18ff., the name of Yahweh is regularly invoked. (Not for nothing is the narrative termed "J.") Yahweh's name is known, used, and honored. But in the speech of the serpent (3:2–5), the primary linguistic characteristic is that God's name is either forgotten, denied, or censored. Four times the serpent speaks about "God," but always in a generic sense and without reference to the name of Yahweh. The result is alienation and fear.

Too much should not be made of that example, especially since it is drawn from a text not on Zimmerli's agenda,[23] but it hints at the urgency of Zimmerli's insight. Everything depends on this self-disclosure of the name of the true sovereign.[24] Where that name is known and given, Israel needs no other aid. Where that name is not given and not known, Israel is lost and hopeless.

Thus the reader is invited to these essays. It seems clear that we shall not exhaust them soon. Our debt is great to John Knox Press for making them available, and I express my thanks to Douglas W. Stott for his translation.

Walter Brueggemann
Eden Theological Seminary

I Am Yahweh

I Am Yahweh

1953

1

In his essay, "The Origins of Israelite Law" (1934), Albrecht Alt showed quite persuasively that from the perspective of form-criticism the Decalogue should be viewed within the context of ancient apodictic commandment series. One of the elements distinguishing it from other such series known to us is the preamble in Exodus 20:2 standing at the beginning of the commandments. Even in the most recent secondary literature a peculiar vacillation continues to characterize both the translation and the interpretation of this statement.

In any case, there can be no doubt that the second part of the statement contains a relative clause offering a more specific qualification of the preceding name of God: ". . . who brought you out of the land of Egypt, out of the house of bondage" (rsv). Should we follow the Septuagint[1] and translate the first half as "I am Yahweh your God," or should we take *yhwh* to be a mere apposition and translate accordingly, "I, Yahweh, am your God"?[2] Or should we, with Poebel, understand the statement as part of the entire First Commandment and translate: "Besides me, Yahweh, your God, who brought you . . . you shall have no other gods"?[3] Of the three interpretations, the first apparently gives us a statement of self-introduction. An unnamed someone steps out of that unknown state by revealing his personal name, by making it recognizable. The most important element here is the disclosure of Yahweh's personal name, a name containing the full richness and honor of the

One naming himself.[4] In the third interpretation, on the other hand, the personal name is totally submerged in the commandment·itself. It now serves incidentally to reaffirm that this God who demands his exclusive seigneurial right is precisely the well-known God appearing immediately thereafter. Finally, the sense of the second translation lies somewhere between the two already mentioned. Here, too, Yahweh is already known by name, and in an introductory statement prior to the commandment he states that he is "your (Israel's) God." This predicate statement contains both a gratuitous element of concern[5] as well as the element of demand and claim, and within the framework of a statement by Yahweh, of course, such a claim is exclusive. Thus although this statement is a syntactically independent nominal clause, it also alludes already to the following first commandment, which is itself formulated as an independent verbal clause.

If we subject these alternatives to a preliminary evaluation, we immediately encounter serious objections to the interpretation represented by Poebel.[6] Although the punctuation he suggests is syntactically possible, it noticeably disturbs the manner of speech used elsewhere in the Decalogue. The discordantly extraneous *casus pendens* (Exod. 20:2) underscores the suffix of the ' *l pny* in the commandment itself, and as an anticipated subject it pushes the commandment formulation of verse 3 into the position of predicate within the complex nominal clause. This is not only aesthetically displeasing, but also destructive of the style of the apodictic prohibition so clearly recognized by Alt. Anyone who, nonetheless, accepts Poebel's interpretation cannot·fail to see that we are dealing at best with a totally secondary expansion of the original form of the commandment. In conformity with other passages, this additional element clearly has a life of its own apart from the parenthetical position it occupies here. Thus our investigation can safely concentrate on an evaluation of the short statement *'nky yhwh 'lhyk*. What can we say about its translation, meaning, and origin?

2

It seems advisable for our exploration of these questions to begin with statements from the Holiness Code. At the top of the legal stipulations in Leviticus 18 we find the thematic nominal clause *' ny yhwh ' lhykm*, a clause echoing the preamble to the Decalogue. Immediately following, though without any conjunction as transition, we find a paraenesis[7] (Lev. 18:3–5). Verse 6, however, begins a series of apodictic commandments formulated in an extremely taut style. Within the Holiness Code we encounter the *' ny yhwh ' lhykm* as a preamble only in 18:2. In the subsequent statements of Leviticus 18—26[8] this statement never again appears as an introduction; it does, however, appear several times as a concluding statement to the commandments or smaller commandment series.

Another finding is that this concluding formula appears in two separate forms. The short form *'ny yhwh* contains only a subject and the predicate of the nominal clause, the latter expressed by a single word. The fuller, longer form *' ny yhwh ' lhykm* corresponds more closely to the Decalogue formulation. Our observations concerning form also reveal that in the majority of cases this formulation has been added asyndetically. Only rarely do we encounter a connnecting *ky*.

If we now inquire as to the translation of the formula, it is clear that the short form can only be translated "I am Yahweh."[9] But should we translate the longer form as "I am Yahweh, your God" or as "I, Yahweh, am your God"? A careful comparison of passages containing the short form with those containing the long form reveals no definite rule governing which form must appear in any given instance. Even a cursory look at chapter 19, for example, can demonstrate this. We might say that the paraenetic statements show a certain preference for the fuller form, though we also encounter the short form in such passages. Similarly, we encounter both the long and the short form within the actual commandment statements. All this fosters the strong impression that we are dealing with a somewhat promiscuous employment of the two forms. This in any case prevents us from thinking the two forms might reveal a distinctly different content. They apparently, either in fuller or more succinct form, want to make statements with the same content.

If this conclusion is correct, then we cannot offer different translations for the two formulations, since they both clearly come from the *same* source. For the fuller formulation we can at this point[10] only consider the rendering "I am Yahweh, your God." If we then question further which of the two formulations deserves form-critical priority, the answer is unquestionably the short form. The statement "I am Yahweh" contains the element of self-introduction by means of the use of the personal name in its pure form. The fuller formulation, "I am Yahweh, your God," adds a secondary element to this self-introduction; namely, the statement that the one introducing himself under the name Yahweh also stands in a divine and lordly relationship to the group of people designated in the suffix (to Israel, the people of Yahweh). This second statement apparently does not intend to add an extraneous or new element to the first, but rather intends to be merely the appropriate development of the first. Israel does not know Yahweh except as its God. More precisely: Yahweh never made himself known to Israel except as Israel's God.[11]

At least within the limited sphere of the Holiness Code, we encounter a certain agitation in this proximity of the two forms of the self-introductory phrase in which Yahweh introduces himself by name. More exactly, we can say that Yahweh's statement of self-introduction tends toward development and further explication. We can see more of this in the Holiness Code. By speaking up to this point of only two types of self-introductory phrases, we imprecisely simplified what is actually found in the Holiness Code. In reality the short form can be expanded in several ways. The self-introductory phrase expanded by ' *lhykm*[12] can be enriched further by the reference, in a relative clause, to the fundamental deed of the Exodus in which Yahweh historically showed himself to be Israel's God (Lev. 19:36). To this deed one can then add an anticipation of the giving of the land of Canaan (25:38). One can underscore the liberation from the yoke of slavery effected by this leading out (26:13) or speak of the meaning of this deed as a separation from the other peoples of Canaan (20:24). Another possibility is to use participial additions to show just who this Yahweh is who makes himself known in his name. He is the one who sanctifies his people and priests (20:8; 21:15, 23; 22:9, 16) and leads them out of Egypt in order to be their God (22:32f.),[13] indeed, in order to dwell in their midst (as is the case outside the Holiness Code in Exod. 29:46 and Num. 35:34).

This kind of extensive amplification of the basic formula of self-introduction finally bursts its original grammatical framework; what was originally an additional attributive statement attached to the name of Yahweh now receives the full weight of an independent predicate. Should one translate ' ny yhwh mqdšm as "I am Yahweh, who sanctifies them," or as "I, Yahweh, sanctify them"?[14] The disintegration of the original phrase of self-introduction has clearly taken place wherever, on the one hand, the statement predicating the name of Yahweh has as an emphatic predicate been placed at the beginning of the entire self-introductory phrase and, on the other hand, Yahweh's name has been degraded to the status of an attribute of the subject: "I, Yahweh, your God, am holy" (qdwš ' ny yhwh ' lhykm in Lev. 19:2; cf. 20:26; 21:8; perhaps also 20:7c LXX).[15]

In Ezekiel, a book related to the Holiness Code, we find the same agitation and varied interpretive possibilities concerning the formulaic phrase of self-introduction, even though we find the pure self-introductory formula only in chapter 20 (which will be considered later). Otherwise we encounter it exclusively as a component in the extended statement, "You will know that I am Yahweh." We will refer to this in the following discussion as the *statement of recognition*. In the short formula we believe we can recognize the process of Yahweh's self-introduction. In the extended statement of recognition this process has been made into the object of human recognition or knowledge, recognition which itself emerges, usually at the conclusion of larger speech units, as the intended goal of Yahweh's activity. Yahweh acts, judges, and is merciful so that his people or people at large (the subject can vary) will know that "I am Yahweh." In view of this peculiarly angular formulation in which a nominal clause with Yahweh's "I" as the subject surprisingly appears as the object clause, we naturally ask why all this could not be expressed much more simply with the statement, "They will know me." And indeed, we find that formulation in Ezekiel 38:16.[16] Thus the extended statement of recognition is not a result of the author being unable to formulate it in this way. However, this smooth manner of speech occurs only once in Ezekiel, whereas the more complex formulation occurs in the overwhelming majority of cases; this preference can only be the result of the forceful effect of the fixed formula of self-introduction, whose powerful content is supposed to resound in the statement of recognition.

We initially encounter the same variations of the self-introductory formula enclosed within the statement of recognition as we did in the Holiness Code. The formula can be expanded by adding the nominal suffix ' *lhyhm*: "They will know that I am Yahweh, their God." It can be expanded by a participle that often clearly bursts the structure of the short formula and usurps the function of the predicate, so that the Yahweh name becomes an attribute of the subject: "Then you will know that I, Yahweh, smite" (7:9); "Then the nations will know that I, Yahweh, sanctify Israel" (37:28, RSV; cf. 20:12). The same thing occurs in the adjectival expansions that remind us of those in the Holiness Code: "And the nations shall know that I, Yahweh, am the Holy One in Israel" (39:7). However, we should not forget that despite this rupturing of the syntactical form, the old formula of self-introduction echoes through; these translations are by no means able to reproduce the full import and content of the Hebraic formulation with all its implications.

We would find the same thing happening wherever expansion by means of a finite verb has ruptured the old nominal formula and the ' *ny yhwh* has apparently become something quite different. The effect of the formula of self-introduction, the emphatic gravity it gives a statement, is still discernable in the recurring formulations: "They shall know that I, Yahweh, have spoken in my jealousy" (5:13, RSV), ". . . that I, Yahweh have not spoken in vain" (6:10), ". . . that I, Yahweh, have drawn my sword out of its sheath" (21:5, RSV), and elsewhere. This is also the context in which we find the statement used so absolutely at the conclusion of a speech: "I, Yahweh, have spoken," a statement that in some passages underscores the validity of the speech still further by adding "and I will do it."[17] Beginning this short concluding statement with the words of the formula of self-introduction emphasizes in an extremely strong fashion Yahweh's "I" coming from Yahweh's own mouth. The Lord himself, in his full personality, speaks in place of the messenger who normally delivers the concluding formula *n'm yhwh*.

Whereas in the passages just cited we can recognize the beginning disintegration of the formula of self-introduction, at the exact opposite end of the spectrum we find it rigidly self-contained and encapsulated. Thrust like an erratic block into a fluid sentence structure, it can throw this unique ego—the "I" of Yahweh that makes itself heard most distinctly in its self-introduction—into abrupt relief. We hear in Numbers 3:41, "I take for myself—I am Yahweh—the Levites instead of all the first-born among the people of Israel."[18] The formula of self-introduction has completely lost its original life here and in this petrification has become a powerfully emphasized "I" in the mouth of Yahweh.

3

Where did the formula of self-introduction have its original life? What did it mean in that original setting? We are fortunate enough to hear an extremely precise answer to this question from within the Priestly literature, to which we will for the moment consciously limit our investigation. In this context the narrative (Priestly Writing) and the prophetic priest (Ezekiel) complement one another and vivify the background against which we can view the employment of the formula of self-introduction within the framework of legal discussion.

Exodus 6 is the first place the formula appears in the Priestly narrative. The passage makes it perfectly clear that this is not merely an incidental use of the formula of self-introduction, even though it is the first such use. A fully conscious theological reflection has placed the formula precisely here first. It cannot appropriately appear any earlier, nor can it appropriately go silent now that it has appeared. Exodus 6 integrates the self-introductory formula into the framework of a larger historico-theological vision. "And God said to Moses, 'I am Yahweh. I appeared to Abraham, to Isaac, and to Jacob, as (under the name) El Shaddai,[19] but by my name Yahweh I did not make myself known to them (I did not reveal myself)' " (vss. 2–3). Then there follows a reference to the covenant with the patriarchs and to the content of the promise, content to be fulfilled in answer to the cries of the afflicted Israelites in Egypt. In the hour of Moses' calling, this fulfillment is compressed into the particular task given him; the announcement itself is framed both at beginning and end by the formula of self-introduction. Furthermore, as the announcement continues, it offers the *'ny yhwh* yet again at a critical juncture imbedded in the statement of recognition:

> Say therefore to the people of Israel, "I am Yahweh, and I will bring you out from under the burdens of the Egyptians, and I will deliver you from their bondage, and I will redeem you with an outstretched arm and with great acts of judgment, and I will take you for my people, and I will be your God; and you shall know that I am Yahweh, your God, who has brought you out from under the burdens of the Egyptians. And I will bring you into the land which I swore to give to Abraham, to Isaac, and to Jacob; I will give it to you for a possession. I am Yahweh." (Exod. 6:6–8, RSV)

It would be wise now, immediately after this account of the Priestly narrator, to examine the historical recapitulation in Ezekiel 20. The relationship between the two accounts is unmistakable.

> On the day when I chose Israel, I swore to the seed of the house of Jacob, making myself known to them (revealed myself to them) in the land of Egypt, I swore to them, saying, I am Yahweh, your God. On that day I swore to them that I would bring them out of the land of Egypt into a land that I had searched out for them, a land flowing with milk and honey, the most glorious of all lands. And I said to them, Cast away the detestable things your eyes feast on, every one of you, and do not defile yourselves with the idols of Egypt; I am Yahweh, your God. (20:5–7, RSV)

An initial comparison of these two formulations of the same traditional material uncovers two fundamental differences. Ezekiel 20 contains no reference at all to the patriarchal tradition.[20] It offers the basic Israelite tradition in the form of the "small historical Credo" (von Rad) and as a result, in contrast to the Pentateuch narratives, sounds extremely archaic. On the other hand, the formulation in Ezekiel shows us a daring "modernization" in the slurring of the traditions in a way we encounter nowhere outside the book of Ezekiel. Within an important sequence the giving of the

Law is woven totally into the departure period of the Exodus story. What in the older tradition followed by P is separated into two event sequences—the leading out of Egypt (with the preceding call of Moses and attendant revelation of the name of Yahweh) and the events at the mountain of God—is in Ezekiel 20 concentrated and tautly integrated by the prophet into the initial introductory encounter of Yahweh with his people. The first and second commandments of the Decalogue appear with pointed relevancy in the command to cast away "the detestable things your eyes feast on" and the "idols of Egypt" (20:7, RSV).[21] The usual tradition then determines the remaining presentation of the history of the people. Within the framework of the desert wanderings we hear more about the giving of the Law. In a peculiar stylization that actually retards the accelerating intensity of the chapter's overall tempo, the first desert generation is given the good statutes and ordinances "by whose observance man shall live" (20:11, RSV); moreover, they are given the sabbaths. To the second generation, on the other hand, is given the "statutes that were not good and ordinances by which they could not have life" (20:25, RSV).[22]

For our investigation it is more significant that Ezekiel 20, like Exodus 6, shifts the revelation to Israel as it is departing from Egypt so that this revelation now stands under the auspices of the formula of self-introduction. The result is that here, too, the phrase "I am Yahweh" carries all the weight and becomes the denominator upon which all else rests. Our interpretation may then assert that everything Yahweh has to announce to his people appears as an amplification of the fundamental statement, "I am Yahweh."

This amplification does not, however, occur in exactly the same way in the two passages. It is, above all, common both to Exodus 6 and to Ezekiel 20 that they place the formula of self-introduction in a totally absolute fashion at the beginning as the truly fundamental message, Exodus 6 using the original short form, Ezekiel 20 the expanded form with 'lhykm. Exodus 6 develops the new element in this self-conveyance by referring to the earlier divine revelation under the name 'l šdy. The commission to Moses beginning in verse 6, telling him to go and speak to the people under the auspices of both an introductory and concluding 'ny yhwh, essentially contains

the portrayal of the impending divine action that will mean the
fulfillment of the promise to the fathers. The most profound
intention of the divine action on behalf of the people will be fulfilled
when the following insight emerges: "You shall know that I am
Yahweh" (6:7). In this final statement we again stand before the
event in which the name is revealed. The entire historical task of
leadership to which Moses is commissioned draws its God-willed
significance not only from subsequent events, but also from the
impact of precisely this fundamental, revelatory truth: the
knowledge of Yahweh's name as an event of Yahweh's self-introduction.

Ezekiel 20, on the other hand, lacks any reference to earlier
stages of a revelation of names. In place of this, however, the
preambular pronouncement of Yahweh's name is explicated by two
important categories of interpretation. "I swore to the seed of the
house of Jacob and revealed myself to them" (20:5). And as if it had
to be underscored in order to bring the full weight of the statement
to bear, the passage repeats: "I swore to them, saying, I am
Yahweh, your God" (20:5, RSV). The interpretation of Yahweh's
self-introduction employs two categories. The self-introduction is a
self-revelation; it discloses something previously unknown to the
illumination of full recognition. The following statements also make
it clear that Ezekiel shares the view of Exodus 6:7 that this
revelation calls the people (and the surrounding peoples) into a
movement of recognition that is not a state of enraptured vision, but
rather is life, activity, and movement toward a goal. And the goal of
this recognition can only be described with the formula of the initial
revelation: "They shall know that I am Yahweh." Even though the
account of Ezekiel (and of P) shows this process of recognition
moving through events (experiences of salvation and catastrophes
of judgment), its goal is not some objective, historical state of
affairs, but rather is the recognition of Yahweh's self-revelation
precisely in his name. Recognition of Yahweh thus occurs "from
knowing to knowing."

We turn now to the second category, the one particularly
emphasized by repetition. "I swore to them, saying, I am Yahweh,
your God" (20:5, RSV). Yahweh's self-introduction is qualified as an

oath. Now, an oath is the action that establishes the binding validity of what is spoken between two parties by invoking a third party who is overseeing the exchange (and who in this case can be none other than Yahweh himself). An oath is a promise of loyalty that is verified by witnesses. The 'ny yhwh, Yahweh's self-introduction, is thus qualified as an event of loyalty. This revelation of Yahweh's name is a revealing of Yahweh himself; it comes to certain people, binds itself to them, and for the sake of its oath remains loyal to them. It is not to be viewed as a distant light standing in the heavens, but rather as a gift to be received, as one receives grace. It intends to be grasped, as one grasps a hand. This explains why Ezekiel does not employ the short basic formula, but rather the formula of self-introduction expanded and interpreted by the substantive attribute. "I am Yahweh, your God." This expresses explicitly the transitive nature of Yahweh's fundamental revelation to Israel. The juxtaposition of Ezekiel 20 and Exodus 6 allows us to add definitively that in Ezekiel, too, Yahweh's self-introduction in the mystery of his name stands at the center. It is thus no accident that throughout the following story related by Ezekiel 20 Yahweh's attention to his own name becomes the real dynamic behind the story. "And you shall know that I am Yahweh, when I deal with you for my name's sake" (20:44, RSV).[23] The statements in verse 5, statements showing a surprising level of theological abstraction, are followed by the more concrete developments in verses 6f. Yahweh's oath promises a concrete history of merciful guidance. "On that day I swore to them that I would bring them out of the land of Egypt into a land that I had searched out for them, a land flowing with milk and honey, the most glorious of all lands" (20:6, RSV).[24] Yahweh's history with Israel is the place where the truth of his revelatory word becomes recognizable in its unfolding.

To this promise of guidance is added the commandment as a second element. The formulation makes it quite clear that this, too, is understood as emerging directly from Yahweh's self-introduction. "And I said to them, Cast away the detestable things your eyes feast on, every one of you, and do not defile yourselves with the idols of Egypt; I am Yahweh, your God (20:7, RSV)." Yahweh's self-revelation, interpreted as an oath, contains Yahweh's direct

command to his people to extricate themselves from every
connection with other gods. This formulation, however, now also
leads us into the context of the legal formulations of the Holiness
Code, where we find the peculiar, usually asyndetic appearance of
the formula of self-introduction behind the commandment to be a
fixed and regular occurrence.[25] This enables us to discern the proper
placement of these peculiar legal formulations according to the
self-understanding of the Priestly tradition. A comparison of the
Holiness Code with Ezekiel 20:7 makes it clear that this
indefatigable repetition of 'ny yhwh at the end of individual
statements or smaller groups of statements in the legal offerings is
not to be understood as thoughtlessly strewn decoration; rather,
this repetition pushes these legal statements into the most central
position from which the Old Testament can make any statement.
Each of these small groups of legal maxims thereby becomes a legal
communication out of the heart of the Old Testament revelation of
Yahweh. Each one of these small units offers in its own way a bit of
explication of the central self-introduction of Yahweh, the God who
summons his people—or better, recalling Leviticus 18 ff. (and
Ezek. 20), the God who sanctifies his people.[26]

The underscoring of one important insight that in another
direction can round off our findings to a full contextual whole is still
missing. A peculiar two-phase process in Yahweh's self-introduction is noticeable in Exodus 6. Verses 2–5 recount Yahweh's
introduction in his revelation to Moses, while verses 6 ff. present the
commission with which Moses is sent to the people. Not only is the
human mediator Moses told to deliver his message to the people,
but the introductory 'ny yhwh is also expressly placed at the
beginning of the message with which Yahweh commissions him.
The messenger is advised to speak in the style of revelation under
the auspices of the formula of self-introduction. We thus see quite
clearly two completely different occasions in which the 'ny yhwh is
heard: (1) in the mouth of Yahweh in the hour of actual divine
encounter; (2) in the subsequent hour growing out of the first
revelation, when the person commissioned extends the message to
the people. Exodus 6 shows that the 'ny yhwh is also completely
legitimate within the mediate occurrence between the person

commissioned and the congregation addressed. Whereas Exodus 6:6 ff. initially focuses on only the delivery of the "gospel" of the liberation from Egypt, the framing introductory formulas in the Holiness Code show this process from the perspective of the giving of the commandments. Nowhere in the latter do we hear of any direct address of the community by Yahweh. They always allude to the speech of Yahweh's commissioned mediator who is speaking either to a larger or smaller circle of the people of God. "And Yahweh said to Moses, 'Say to the people of Israel, I am Yahweh . . .' " (Lev. 18:1, RSV).[27]

This collective consideration of the priestly statements in P, the Holiness Code, and Ezekiel leads us unmistakably to a liturgical procedure in which a speaker with the authority of divine commissioning delivers to the community words of the most serious import. Both the account of Yahweh's saving deeds in history as well as the mediation of the divine maxims are placed under the introductory and concluding formula of Yahweh's self-introduction that is to be spoken with full authority by the person commissioned. Further, Ezekiel 20 also betrays an attitude according to which virtually all the decisive elements of the revelation are already contained within Yahweh's revelation of his name. Although we cannot discuss it further at this time, questions about Yahweh's name and about the blessing of the people in the name of Yahweh are considerably illuminated from this perspective.

4

Up to this point we have strictly limited our investigation to the general circle of Priestly statements, statements doubtlessly issuing from a stage of extreme reflective maturity. We must now expand the investigation to include the entire Old Testament, and it may be that the general findings of our survey will prove to be surprising. Although we encounter the formula of self-introduction with extreme frequency in the priestly writing both as an independent statement and as one imbedded in the statement of recognition, except for its frequent employment by Deutero-Isaiah—with which we will have to deal particularly—the formula occurs only rarely in the rest of the Old Testament writings. In the following discussion we will no longer deal extensively with the statement of recognition, since a full exploration of it is beyond the scope of the present study.[28] In the above discussion of the Priestly texts we made several fundamental remarks concerning it that will be important to the context of our argument.

In its pure form[29] we encounter the formula of self-introduction appropriately—given its fundamental nature—within the narrative literature in the accounts of the theophanies in Genesis and Exodus. It will be advantageous for us to consider also the Elohistic passages which do not yet contain the name Yahweh, since they are of significance for the characterization of the formula of self-introduction. After excluding the Priestly passages Genesis 17:1 ff.; 35:11; and Exodus 6:2 ff., we need to consider the following: Genesis 15:7 (J); 26:24 (J—secondary?); 28:13 (J); 31:11 ff. (E) 'ml'k·h'lhym; 46:3 (E); Exodus 3:6 (E); cf. also Joshua 5:14. Usually God encounters humans here with consolation or encouraging promises. This is the case with Isaac as he wanders about pursued by Abimelech's servants; with Jacob during his flight from Esau, later from Laban, and at the time of his departure to Egypt; and with Moses during the time of his people's afflictions.

Except in Genesis 31, God's self-introduction precedes the actual revelatory speech. In the Elohistic formulations in 31:11 ff.; 46:3; and Exodus 3:6 there is an introductory call by God, to which the human responds with his *hnny*. Twice we hear the consoling "fear not" (Gen. 26:24; 46:3). For the rest, God introduces himself as the familiar one by referring to things already known or things that have already taken place. We hear the consoling idea of the loyalty of this God in his action and in his promise. He is known as the God who led Abraham away from Ur (Gen. 15:7), the God of Bethel (Gen. 31:13), the God of the father of Isaac (Gen. 26:24), of Jacob (Gen. 46:3), the God of Abraham and of Isaac (Gen. 28:13), and in Exodus 3:6 in comprehensive fashion as the God of the three fathers. The content of these theophanies is never the proclamation of law, but rather the promise of imminent help and guidance that prompt certain decisions on the part of human beings (Jacob's departure from Laban, journey to Egypt, departure from Egypt). We sense the weight of a certain solemnity in Genesis 15, a chapter that looks beyond the exigencies of the moment toward the establishment of a secure covenantal relationship. Is it merely coincidental that precisely here we encounter an allusion to the Exodus formulation "who brought you from . . ."?

In none of these passages does the formula of self-introduction have the constitutive significance of the Priestly *'ny yhwh* formula, which can imply an entire liturgical event and a presentation of legal material. Rather, we need to ask about the experiential horizon that has shaped the scenes of divine encounter to which these statements belong. Begrich, in the *Zeitung für Alttestamentliche Wissenschaft* 52 (1934), disclosed the liturgical form of the oracle of favorable supplication-hearing. The "fear not" and "I am with you," as well as the concrete promise of request bestowal and of coming help, are all anchored in this kind of oracle which the priest speaks with full authority to the suppliant. In the classical prayer literature of the Fertile Crescent, we find the clearest example of this form of oracular supplication answer in a prayer spoken by Ashurbanipal to Nabu and in the following extended answer from Nabu.[30] The form disclosed by Begrich, like the answer of Nabu, does not contain the element of divine self-introduction. In contrast, the oracles given to and carefully collected by Esarhaddon contain a type of divine answer that is at least formally related to this first type; the difference is that in the latter the formula of divine self-introduction recurs with fixed regularity.

> I am Ishtar of Arbela, O Esarhaddon king of Assyria. In the cities of Ashur, Nineveh, Calah, Arbela, protracted days, everlasting years, unto Esarhaddon my king shall I grant. I am your great protector (?). Your gracious leader am I. . . . "Fear not, O king," I said to you, "I have not abandoned you." I have given you confidence, I shall not let you be disgraced.[31]

The priority of divine self-introduction we find in this citation is by no means a fixed rule in other passages, rather it seems that a great deal of freedom is being exercised here. Nonetheless, we can hardly fail to recognize the typological kinship of the overall divine discourse. In addition to the form of promised request bestowal disclosed by Begrich (the form without a formula of self-introduction), was there in Israel also the form that did contain that formula?

The passages from Genesis and Exodus suggest as much. The significant objective difference between the two examples would then be primarily that the promises to Esarhaddon are not part of a larger promissory history encompassing several generations, but rather are more distinctly occasional. In the statement "your gracious leader am I" (*mu-še-ṣu-ta-ka*) we do not find the same historical resonance as in the "who brought you from Ur" of Genesis 15:7 and in the echoing "who brought you out of Egypt."

5

The letters from Mari have introduced us to yet another type of divine decree from the Fertile Crescent. W. von Soden[32] has questioned whether the *muḫḫûm*, the proclaimer of this kind of decree, is not a person different from the normal priest and more similar to the biblical prophet. In von Soden's examples, the *muḫḫûm*'s divine decree commences without any distinct formula of divine introduction. Only in the Mari letter that Lods and Dossin present in the collection for Th. Robinson[33] do we find a formula of self-introduction, though significantly in the striking form of a question. "Adad spoke in oracles, the lord of Kallassu, in the following way: Am I not Adad, lord of Kallassu, who reared him [Zimrilim] in my lap . . . ?"[34] Should we then suspect that the divine discourses of the Mari prophets also show signs of a discursive form in which the divine speech is itself introduced by divine self-introduction? What do we find regarding this in Old Testament prophecy?

A comparative glance at divine discourse in Old Testament prophecy discloses an extremely unambiguous picture. In the older written prophets—Isaiah, Amos, and Micah—we encounter absolute silence regarding the formula of self-introduction. Not once in the words of these prophets does Yahweh introduce himself in the formula of self-introduction, even though for the most part he speaks in the first person. Of the early prophets only Hosea appears to be an exception to this rule. In two passages (12:9 and 13:4) we find the full formula of divine self-introduction in an extremely weighty form. A closer look, however, reveals clearly that this is by no means a new form of Yahweh's self-introduction originating with the prophet. Rather, the self-statement in both passages recounting Yahweh's great reckoning with his people refers unmistakably to a self-introduction already long known to Israel and recalls it as the reality in which Israel ought to stand. "I am Yahweh, your God from the land of Egypt." On the basis of this salvation relationship, which was already constitutive for the old Credo, God will act anew on Israel's behalf, miraculously recalling past experiences: "I will again make you dwell in tents, as in the days of the appointed feast" (12:9). Thus through the prophetic statement here we see the reflection of Israel's confessional formula that no doubt also stands behind and is altered in the priestly statements.

The similarly structured statement in Hosea 13:4 (RSV) contains a strongly polemical note. "I am Yahweh, your God, from the land of Egypt; you know no God but me, and besides me there is no savior." Yahweh's singularity is thrown into sharp relief here in a kind of hymnic self-praise. Here also, however, we encounter a form of self-statement that is by no means limited only to Israel. In a study of Sumerian and Accadian parallels to the structure of Old Testament psalms (1922), Stummer disclosed among other things the so-called "portrayal of magnificence." As a rule we find this in the mouth of the suppliant, though it can also occur in the mouth of the deity as a kind of self-exaltation. It accordingly conforms to the introductory formula of self-introduction and of divine epiphany.[35]

We must now discuss Deutero-Isaiah. The work of Gressmann,[36] Köhler, Begrich, and others has shown persuasively that Deutero-Isaiah represents a later form of Old Testament prophecy that is influenced by liturgical song even at the level of the material content of the proclamation. Thus the overflowing richness of variation the formula of self-introduction experiences in Deutero-Isaiah should be understood not from the perspective of the old prophetic style, but rather from that of liturgical poetry.

We will first discuss the findings that concern form. Deutero-Isaiah, too, contains passages in which the formula of self-introduction appears in its terse, original form, so that there can be no doubt as to the translation "I am Yahweh." We encounter it both as an independent statement (45:6, 7, 18) and imbedded in the statement of recognition (45:3; 49:23). In 45:21 it has been freely transformed into a rhetorical question of the kind we saw in the Mari letter citation. In 43:11 the subject of the formula of self-introduction has been emphasized by doubling and the use of the more profound sounding *'nky* (*'nky 'nky yhwh*). Within the framework of the statement of recognition, the predicate of the formula in 49:23 has been qualified more specifically in a relative clause. Chapter 45, verse 3 is significant because the formula has been expanded attributively in a grammatically unambiguous fashion by a participle with an article. Here we can only translate: "That you may know that I am Yahweh, the God of Israel, who calls you by your name." However, we also find the formula expanded in Deutero-Isaiah by means of a nondetermined participle. Here the original formulaic structure rearranges itself, and the name Yahweh, displaced from the clear position of predicate, threatens to degenerate into an attribute of the introductory personal pronoun. Should we translate 44:24, "I am Yahweh, who made all things" (as does Volz); or, "I, Yahweh, do all these things" (as does Volz in the analogous passage 45:7); or as would also be the case then with 41:4, "I, Yahweh, am the first, and with the last I am"?[37] In 41:13; 43:3; and 48:17, where we find the suffix complement *'lhym*, should we translate: "I, Yahweh, am your God" or "I am Yahweh, your God"? In 43:15 one sees that the *'lhym* in the sense of the Isaian formula of "the Holy One of Israel" can be replaced by *qdwš yśr'l*, in which case the statement of creation is combined with the expressly mentioned name of Israel in a typically Deutero-Isaian continuation: "I am Yahweh, your Holy One (or: I, Yahweh, am your Holy One?), the Creator of Israel, your King." Considering the hovering character of Deutero-Isaiah's hymnic style in which one predicate quickly pushes aside the next, we cannot really insist in a sharp either-or fashion on a definite syntactical ordering of the name Yahweh. We cannot fail, however, to hear the formula of self-introduction resounding in all these statements, including the purely verbally extended formulations such as 41:17 ("I, Yahweh, answer them") and 42:6 ("I, Yahweh, have called you"). This is expressed quite clearly in 42:8 by the statement "I am Yahweh, that is my name" that both summarizes and underscores the entire context of verses 6–8. Further, the formulations in which *yhwh* is replaced by '*l* are also examples of free variation of the formula of self-introduction: "For I am God, and there is no other" (45:22; 46:9; in 45:5, 6, 18 it is a perfect parallel to the pure formula). The same is true whenever merely a supporting *hw*' is added to the I.[38] This includes in the widest sense also the simple emphatic I-statements. A comparison, for example, of 45:12 f. with 44:24, or of 48:15 with 42:6 and 45:3 shows that these amplified I-statements are also quite appropriately interpreted from the perspective of the formula of self-introduction.[39]

If we inquire further concerning in which literary types and at what point within those types the formula of self-introduction is employed, we are led to two main forms. According to Begrich's genre analysis, we encounter it (1) in the judgment and disputation discourses. Here the formula of self-introduction often prefaces the divine self-assertion with which Yahweh answers the preceding trial questions (41:4; 43:11, 12, 13; 45:18, 21; 48:12).[40] We find it (2) in God's oracular answers to Israel's supplications. Here it functions not only within the concluding statement of recognition giving the purpose of the answer (49:23, 26),[41] but also as the justification for the words of consolation, introduced by *ky* (41:[10]13; 43:3*a*) or merely added asyndetically (43:15, though the first half is somewhat ambiguous). Only in 41:17 and 48:17 does it occur at the head of the supplication answer, and this position may distantly echo the kind of answer Ishtar gave to Esarhaddon. A variation of this usage may possibly be contained in the oracular calling in 42:6, 8 (directed to Yahweh's servant) and in 45:2 f., 5 f., 7 (directed to Cyrus).

These formal and literary historical findings lead us further to the question of content. What kind of content does this frequent use of '*ny* ('*nky*) *yhwh* in Deutero-Isaiah bring to expression? Even a cursory glance at the various passages shows us that Yahweh's self-introduction under his own name in Deutero-Isaiah is far more than merely an introductory altering of the dialogue partner's status as a stranger by revealing the personal name, an introduction making the ensuing dialogue possible. It is a statement laden with final significance and basically self-contained; this, of course, recalls the employment of the formula of self-introduction within the Priestly writings. In this self-introduction we hear the ultimate statement Yahweh can make about himself. A glance at parallel statements can greatly illuminate its content.

In all the passages where the formula of self-introduction appears in its short, two-part form, Yahweh's self-exaltation is spoken as a delimitation against potential rival gods. The statement thus moves into the context of similar hymnic statements also found among Israel's neighbors which contain a deity's self-exaltation. Among humans, too, the name is the word that signifies the indelible uniqueness and personal independence of the one who discloses that name. Since Israel's faith recognizes no other comparable deity that might be considered his partner in the divine world, Yahweh's self-introduction thus raises this element to its highest power and gives it a hard, polemical edge. "I am Yahweh, that is my name; my glory I give to no other, nor my praise to graven images" (42:8, RSV). "I am Yahweh, and there is no other, besides me there is no God" (45:5, RSV).[42] This also includes the omnipotent embracing of time that ruptures the syntactical framework of the formula of self-introduction: "I, Yahweh, am the first, and with the last am I ['ny hw']" (41:4, also 44:6, RSV).

However, what in relation to idols was a staunch polemical self-assertion, becomes in the words to Israel a merciful, promissory word of consolation. Even within the context of the pure formula of self-introduction, the soft speech of oracular answer can flow directly into elevated hymnic self-exaltation. "I, I am Yahweh, and besides me there is no savior" (43:11, RSV). "Am I not Yahweh, and there is no other god besides me, a righteous God and a Savior; there is none besides me" (45:21). This is particularly strong wherever Yahweh's name is characterized more closely only by means of a relative clause. "You will know that I am Yahweh, with whom those who wait for me shall not be put to shame" (49:23). For the rest, this accent will naturally be thrown into especially sharp relief whenever (as was already the case in the Holiness Code) the short formula of self-introduction is expanded by the addition of 'lhyk addressing Israel. In this case the formula is often added to the supplication answer as further justification and connected by means of ky. "For I am Yahweh, your God, who holds your right hand, who says to you: 'Fear not, I have helped you' "(41:13). "For I am

Yahweh, your God, the Holy One of Israel, your Savior" (43:3a, 43, rsv; according to Begrich, at the conclusion of a first stanza).[43] It stands as an introduction in 48:17, while 51:15 more strongly emphasizes the assertion of might.

It is striking that Deutero-Isaiah nowhere amplifies the formula of self-introduction with the old credal Yahweh predication we heard in Hosea: "Yahweh, who brought you up from Egypt." The old formulas no doubt also resound in Yahweh's I-statements: "Yahweh, the God of Israel" (in 41:17 and 45:3 it is woven in the fashion of a garland into the verse's two parallel halves). The Isaian equivalent is "the Holy One of Israel" (41:14, 16; 43:3, 15–14), or "the Mighty one of Jacob" (49:26).[44] Yahweh's self-designation with reference to the guidance out of Egypt might be missing here because Yahweh's greatest deed from the early period, the deed to which he frequently refers in his self-predication (always in disintegrated formulas), is creation. In 51:9 characteristics of the events at the Reed Sea emerge from the portrayal of the mighty deed of creation. In contrast, the actual Exodus deed to which Deutero-Isaiah refers still lies in the future, and reference to the former Exodus from Egypt recedes behind this future Exodus (43:16 ff.). Thus Yahweh's entire predication in his self-statements is directed decisively toward the Creator's activity that begins in the present and comes to completion in the future; even the creation statement must occasionally bear a future-oriented characterization (41:20; 45:8). Thus all these words of consolation to the exiled Israel are sounded in Yahweh's extended I-statements. He strengthens, helps, grasps both Israel and its appointed liberator Cyrus by the hand, he answers supplications, removes sins, destroys the signs of the soothsayers, and fulfills his word.

We can quickly examine the remaining prophetic passages. We find Deutero-Isaiah's manner of speech in a citation in Isaiah 60:16. The gloss in Zechariah 10:6 recalls Isaiah 41:17. Joel 2:27 (and Deut. 32:39) also echoes Deutero-Isaiah's speech. Isaiah 60:22 recalls the words from Ezekiel, 'ny yhwh dbrty w'śyty. Isaiah 61:8 and Jeremiah 17:10 are formally related by the participial expansion of the formula of self-introduction;[45] as regards content, they both seek to ascertain Yahweh's legal will in hymnic self-statements ("I,

Yahweh, search the mind and try the heart . . . I, Yahweh, love justice"). In Exodus 20:5 we will again encounter this kind of descriptive predication of the God who protects justice. The awkward juxtaposition of accusative and nominative clauses in the statement of recognition in Jeremiah 24:7 shows that this passage is a later product. In Jeremiah 32:27 as well, the dawning of the divine answer to Jeremiah's prayer, the old formula of self-introduction, glimmers through in the theophany. Here, too, however, the pure form has been dismembered. By mentioning the expanded statement of recognition in Joel 4:17 we exhaust the remaining prophetic passages without having found anything essentially new.

The overall picture is clear. The formula of self-introduction does not have any *Sitz im Leben* of its own in prophetic speech. Its frequent appearances in Ezekiel are not a constituent part of Ezekiel's fundamental prophetic characteristics, but rather direct our attention back to his Priestly heritage. The occurrences and allusions in Deutero-Isaiah emerge from the liturgical speech of Yahweh's self-exaltation and of oracular supplication answers. The passages in Hosea reflect Israel's early credal formulations, and the rest of the prophetic passages, as regards form, contain secondary material. It is clear that the prophets, who do indeed experience their central orientation from an encounter with God, nonetheless do not experience this encounter in the kind of theophany (with its "I am" introduction) described by the older tradition. The situation of a prophetic reception and encounter is different than that in which God appears and speaks at the time of the making of the covenant and the giving of the Law, the latter being continually renewed in the liturgical proclamation of the Law.

It is not surprising, of course, that this formula is totally absent in Wisdom, since Wisdom essentially deals with human opinions. Jeremiah 17:10 shows the insertion of divine first-person speech into a mosaic-like structure.

6

The conclusion of our excursion through the Old Testament returns us to the point of departure. Three passages not belonging to the Priestly source can contribute some significant elements to the evaluation of our initial questions by showing us a unique employment of the Decalogue.

The first of these passages, Judges 6:10, again shows us clearly that the formula of self-introduction, as far as its origins and genre are concerned, is easily distinguished from the divine first-person speech of the prophets. According to this Deuteronomic account an unknown prophet ('yš nby'), whom Yahweh has sent to the people (šlḥ), shows the people their disobedience. The divine speech, given in the first person, is in a formal sense correctly introduced by the messenger formula. The content of this reprimand is initially a reference to the great deed expressed in Israel's Credo—the leading out of Egypt to another land—presented in five parallel verbal clauses. Only then is the divine commandment mentioned—noticeably late, compared with the sequence of events given in the Pentateuch tradition. The first Decalogue commandment, standing unmistakably behind the entire formulation, is actualized to involve the gods of Canaan, the conquered land. "And I said to you, 'I am Yahweh, your God; you shall not pay reverence to the gods of the Amorites, in whose land you dwell' " (6:10, RSV).[46] The entire passage in verses 8–10 offers what is virtually an ideal opportunity to place the formula of self-introduction at the beginning of the prophetic speech. The phrase "I led you up from Egypt, and brought you out of the house of bondage," beginning with the emphatic 'nky, practically invites one to formulate the entire Decalogue preamble. It is all the more striking that the formula of self-introduction is not used even though Yahweh's speech begins in first person. It clearly does not belong in the genre of prophetic speech. In contrast, it does indeed belong in the context of the mediation of legal maxims, the context given with verse 10. This decisively controverts the suggestion by Mowinckel,[47] among others, that the legal proclamation was given by the cult prophets at the great festival. Legal proclamation and prophetic speech should be clearly distinguished from one another.

The information yielded by Psalms 50 and 81 is even more significant. It has long been recognized[48] that we can discern here the structure of a liturgical proceeding at whose center stands a divine conveyance of the Decalogue. Both psalms contain the

juxtaposition of the formula of self-introduction and the commandment (expanded in Psalm 81 by a reference to the departure
from Egypt). We recognize commandments six through eight in
50:18 ff., and the first commandment in 81:10. The cry in 50:7 and
81:9 also underscores the kinship between the two psalms.

These psalms yield some concluding insights for our look at the
Decalogue. First, Psalm 50:7 allows us to assert with some certainty
that the preamble to the Decalogue, as already suggested by the
analogous Priestly formulations, should be translated: "I am
Yahweh, your God" and not "I, Yahweh, am your God." This
reversal of predicate and subject in the nominal clause is intended to
accentuate the Yahweh name (a name replaced by 'lhym within the
framework of the Elohistic Psalter) and allows us to ascertain the
subject and predicate with unambiguous clarity. yhwh 'lhyk 'nky
can only be translated: "I am Yahweh, your God."[49] Thus the
formula of self-introduction lies behind or as the basis of not only
the Holiness Code, but the Decalogue as well. The vacillation in the
translation of the preamble ought now to disappear from scholarly
discussion.

We come now to the second point. In Psalm 50 the divine
formula of self-introduction immediately follows the cry, "Hear, O
my people," and this cry is itself followed by Yahweh's speech of
reckoning, a speech whose second part (verses 16 ff.) presupposes
the Decalogue commandments. Psalm 81, on the other hand, recalls
the formulations of the Holiness Code. Here the divine discourse
begins with an enumeration of the great events of liberation from
servitude and of guidance in the desert. The cry, "Hear, O my
people," is then followed by the proclamation of the First
Commandment, which is itself underscored by the asyndetically
inserted formula of self-introduction: "There shall be no strange
god among you; you shall not bow down to a foreign god. I am
Yahweh, your God, who brought you up out of the land of Egypt"
(81:9-10, RSV).[50] These verses demonstrate that even within the
context of the Decalogue the formula of self-introduction maintains
the same mobility we saw in the Priestly formulations and that it can
even move from the beginning to the end of the mediation of
maxims. In conclusion now we need to recognize that the

significance of this is more than merely formal. A statement of self-introduction, as long as it is strictly understood as such, belongs at the top of a discourse; in that position it lends the speaker the quality of familiarity that smooths the way for subsequent communication. The appearance of the formula of self-introduction at the end reveals that something else is at work in the statement. It carries something of the weight of a legitimation. If what it contains is to be brought to unambiguously clear expression, then the conjuction of the causal phrase is added accordingly: "There shall be no strange god among you . . . *for* I am Yahweh, your God." Psalm 81 still speaks in the strict style of asyndetical addition in which the entire majesty of the person freely revealing the self in the personal name is preserved. The possibility of a change in position, however, shows that the preamble to the Decalogue does indeed contain this element of inner legitimation that we found so extensively developed in the Priestly formulations, particularly in Ezekiel 20. The Decalogue itself is already oriented toward the recognition that only in Yahweh's name does one find the legitimate basis not only for his salvation activity, but for his giving of commandments as well.[51]

This leads to our next insight concerning the Decalogue. Within the active history of growth resulting in the form of the Decalogue before us today, the First and Second Commandments—apparently understood as a contextual unity[52]—acquired an additional element. H. Schmidt's suggestion that this was the original preamble is difficult to support.[53] His idea does, however, quite correctly recognize that at least in essence this element represents a contextual parallel to the preamble. The prohibition of doing obeisance to foreign gods (which probably represents a textual expansion) is followed by the sentence, *'nky yhwh 'lhyk 'l qn'*, itself introduced by *ky*. Should we translate: "For I am Yahweh, your God, a jealous God" or "For I, Yahweh, your God, am a jealous God"? We can probably make two assertions here. (1) This phrase represents an expanded formula of self-introduction much like those we encountered in such profusion in the Holiness Code and elsewhere. We can no longer determine in every instance, however, whether the syntactical framework of the formula of self-introduction has already been ruptured or whether the expansion stays within the framework of the attributive interpretation of Yahweh's name. In any event, whenever the structure has clearly been ruptured—and this is very likely the case here—one must be able to hear at least the latent resonance of the basic formula. (2) The expanded formula of self-introduction here has not been added in the strict, asyndetical style of Psalm 81 and most of the statements in the Holiness Code, but rather in a fragmented style signifying a certain rationalization, appropriately introduced by *ky*. This usage characterizes the sentence form-critically as a later product. Space prohibits us from investigating here the prehistory of this second formula that has been added to the first two commandments during a secondary growth phrase. However, this doubling of the formula of self-introduction so that it frames the initial words of the Decalogue in dual form clearly shows how weighty these elements of Yahweh's self-introduction apparently are within the framework of the giving of the Commandments. Quite the opposite of being empty decoration, they are rather the underlying foundation for the Commandments themselves.

Let us consider one final insight. Psalms 50 and 81 confirm what emerged from within the Priestly statements in Exodus 6 and the Holiness Code. The announcement of the legal maxims of the Decalogue has its *Sitz im Leben* in a liturgical proceeding. We clearly recognize the festal character of Psalms 50:5, 7 ff. and 81:4, 9.

For the rest, however, we find a clear difference between the Priestly and the Psalmic statements. The Priestly statements in P and the Holiness Code differentiate between the giving of the Commandments to Moses on the one hand, and the secondary mediation of the Commandments through Moses to the congregation or to the priests on the other. Whereas Yahweh himself is present in the first situation, we hear nothing of his presence in the second, even though the transmission of the Commandments is to take place expressly under the auspices of the formula of self-introduction. From this perspective, too, the accent in the formula moves imperceptibly from a personal self-introduction of the attendant God to a secondary legitimation of the Commandments by reference to Yahweh's "I." This "I," however, moves into proximity to the people in the mediation of the message commissioned to Moses. Yahweh is present in the authoritative words of the proclaimer of the Commandments.

Psalms 50 and 81, on the other hand, clearly portray this mediation to the community as occurring in the presence of Yahweh himself. Contextually they are thus related to the framing accounts in Exodus 19 f. and Deuteronomy 5 where, similarly, Yahweh himself delivers the Decalogue to the people. Psalm 50 describes Yahweh's advent in terms recalling Exodus 19. Psalm 81:2 ff. calls the community to sing aloud and shout for joy—no doubt to the coming God. Psalm 81:5 lets us glimpse the awesomeness of the one approaching: "I hear a voice I had not known." Within the framework of the festival, of course, the phrase of Yahweh's self-introduction and the mediation of the Commandment is representatively spoken by someone with full virtual authority. Psalm 50, however,[54] describes Yahweh's advent—the divine epiphany—in terms that clearly transcend a mere mediation of words.

Mowinckel, in his stimulating study of the Decalogue, has clearly delineated these terms. He believes that the experience of the epiphany, coming to expression in the formula of self-introduction and reaching its climax in the subsequent covenant renewal, constitutes the actual center of the liturgical proceeding. He considers the mediation of the commandments, on the other hand, to be a secondary outgrowth, probably from the processional ritual. The actual festival event, portrayed in dramatic proceedings, is Yahweh's advent for the sake of enthronement and covenant renewal.[55]

We are not concerned in this discussion with pursuing the extensive problems of the Old Testament cult encountered here. We actually know less about it than many recent studies suggest. We must recognize the danger of a fixed concept of cult, acquired elsewhere, that falsely promises genuine insights.[56] Only the most cautious examinations of the textual detail, particularly including the further examination of the formula-material already available, can take us further.

From the perspective of Psalms 50 and 81 we cannot doubt that the element of epiphany in connection with the formula of self-introduction played a role in Israel's worship.[57] However, we must inquire of Mowinckel's separation of the epiphany from the mediation of the commandments whether an alien concept of cult is not prejudicing the interpretation. The Old Testament text, in a significant number of its statements, has shown us the tenacious cohesion of the formula of self-introduction to the proclamation of maxims. Even in later formulations that subordinate the formula of self-introduction we still find the asyndetical connecting of elements, a connecting unmistakably influenced by older traditions. The use of *ky* for logically smooth transitions only sporadically finds its way into the passages. The juxtaposition of self-introductory formula and legal proclamation occurs with striking frequency in the Priestly writing, and this pairing suggests that the priest indeed occupied a special position in the presentation of maxims. Does all this suggest that a peculiar kind of Old Testament covenant cult consisted precisely in this juxtaposition of the legal proclamation with Yahweh's epiphany—just as, within the narrative sphere, the Sinai traditions so clearly assert? In Israel's surroundings we did indeed find analogous employment of the formula of self-introduction in the oracular supplication answer and in the divine self-exaltation, but we did not find such employment in legal proclamation.[58] As a negative confirmation this would certainly not be unfavorable evidence in support of our hypothesis. Further development within the sphere of Priestly literature lets this element of epiphany recede and even integrates the formula of self-introduction clearly into the more discursive liturgical setting. This should not be understood as a turning away from the original elements, but rather probably as a decisive retrieval of what was already an original aspect of the old cult of Yahweh. Mowinckel's rejection of the *culte de la parole* cannot be maintained in such extreme form.

These considerations concerning the formula of self-introduction, gratefully and cordially offered to Albrecht Alt on the occasion of his seventieth birthday, may serve as a welcome confirmation now of what he recognized in his analysis of the legal tradition concerning the extreme age of the apodictic mediation of maxims in the Yahweh faith.

Knowledge of God
According to the Book of
Ezekiel

1954

The First Letter to Timothy says that God dwells in an unapproachable light (6:16). At the same time, however, the writings of both Testaments are full of statements concerning the proper knowledge of God.

The *aprósiton* of the Letter to Timothy needs no special defense today; our age can say a great deal about the puzzling, often tormenting inaccessibility of God, who wards off every direct attempt to probe his mystery. But what about Scripture's assertion of knowledge of God? From which area does this knowledge arise? How does it come about among created beings? What are we able to know of the mystery of the One who dwells in the unapproachable light?

Exegetes of both Testaments as well as systematic theologians labor to solve this formidable puzzle, and the following investigation does not intend to deal with it in its entire scope. It intends rather to focus on a particular Old Testament exegetical area and to try to uncover there what the biblical word has to say about knowledge of God.[1] After all, the clear exegetical understanding of biblical material will always form the basis for further theological reflection in a church oriented toward the Word. To this extent the following investigation also addresses systematic theologians in hopes of stimulating them to risk fuller cooperation with exegesis.

A simple reference to word statistics can justify the specific focus of the present study on statements found in the book of

Ezekiel concerning knowledge of God. Of the 947 verbal occurrences of the stem *yd'* (to know) listed by Mandelkern's concordance,[2] not less than 99 are found in Ezekiel alone, and virtually all of them concern theologically significant statements. The book of Psalms is a quick second with 93 occurrences,[3] while Job stands in third place with 71.[4] In a purely external fashion, then, the book of Ezekiel distinguishes itself from the rest of the Old Testament by its high concentration of statements concerning the knowledge of God and invites us to examine it more closely.

This rather spiritless statistical fact is not the only thing suggesting the book of Ezekiel might lend itself well to such an investigation. Its strongly formulaic language offers a particularly suitable object for the kind of form-critical and tradition-critical investigation that has been used with such success recently. Accordingly, we must first inquire into the particular characteristics of the statements of knowledge in Ezekiel.

1. The Statement of Recognition in the Book of Ezekiel

Even a preliminary, cursory look at the concordance for the verb *yd'* in the book of Ezekiel yields a bit of information whose tenacious reoccurrence is striking. In the 86 passages in which *yd'* appears in the basic form of Qal, a slightly variable, peculiarly monotonous turn of phrase appears again and again. We encounter the statement, "And you (or you plural, or they) shall know that I am Yahweh."[5] In an additional 18 passages the formula has been expanded. In 9 of them the short object clause, "that I am Yahweh," is verbally expanded,[6] in 5 nominally,[7] and in 3 participially.[8] Finally, in a single instance the predicate is formed by a prepositional phrase.[9]

The formulaic context must also include 6 further cases in which we recognize a similar stylization, even though the strict formulation of the object clause and its content of Yahweh's self-naming ("I am Yahweh") are missing: "And you shall know that I have not done without cause all that I have done in it (Jerusalem)" (14:23). If we compare with this the strict, formally correct, verbally expanded statement in 6:10 ("And they shall know that I, Yahweh, have not said in vain that I would do this evil to them"),[10] it becomes clear that 14:23 must be considered a freer alteration that has emerged on the basis of the fomulaic statement of recognition. Here, too, it is a matter of recognition of Yahweh and of his unique activity.[11]

This overall view of Ezekiel's uses of the Qal of *yd'* yields the astonishing insight that of the 86 total occurrences only 8 passages remain in which the verb can be used more freely,[12] while the rest of the 78 occurrences are bound in greater or lesser measure to the formulaic structure.

In order to be thorough, we need to include within the context of this form of speech one or perhaps two passages in which the verb *yd'* is replaced by *r'h* (to see), a term frequently used as its parallel. Chapter 21, verse 5 reads: "And all flesh shall see that I, Yahweh, have ignited it (the flame)." The verbally expanded object clause of the strict formula of recognition cannot be easily recognized here. Chapter 39, verse 21, on the other hand, shows us the freer alteration into an accusative statement:[13] "And all the nations shall see my judgment which I have executed, and my hand which I have laid on them" (RSV). Verses 22 f. add to this a double statement of recognition referring respectively to Israel and the nations: "The house of Israel shall know that I am Yahweh, their God, from that day forward. And the nations shall know that the house of Israel went into captivity for their iniquity . . ." (RSV). This entire complex is, doubtless, an example of a recognition formulation that has been developed to extreme fullness by using the double expression of seeing-knowing.

From this preliminary, general look at the material under investigation we can draw our first conclusion: one cannot speak of Ezekiel's understanding of "knowledge of God" without first considering the uniqueness and origin of this rigidly fixed formulation. That it must somewhere have a life of its own is shown by the tenacity with which it asserts itself; by its marked tendency to allow variations to occur only in a way clearly preserving the basic formulaic content and augmenting the sentence only at its end; by the energy with which it is able to generate analogous formations with the verb *r'h*. What is the origin of this dominate formulation in the book of Ezekiel, one that is so often repeated, variously altered,

and expanded in so many different directions? Can we discover
something more specific about its emergence or about the particular
life-situation to which it belonged? Does it originate with Ezekiel
and the circle associated with his book?[14] Or can we find it in
material predating Ezekiel?

It is probably advisable to spend a bit more time with the book
of Ezekiel before going beyond it and pursuing these questions
further within the Old Testament. Does our understanding of the
recognition formula here already encompass the entire context of
the sphere it determines? It may be that the formula sinks its roots
more deeply into the surrounding textual complex and that the turn
of phrase we encounter here, a phrase never occurring by itself,
manifests a particular relationship to its overall context. In that case
the formula in all its uniqueness would only be fully delineated by
disclosing its relationship to the surrounding textual material. Can
we find something of this in the book of Ezekiel?

2. The Formal and Content-oriented Relationship Between the Statement of Recognition and Its Context in the Book of Ezekiel

In answer to this question let us examine three typical uses of
the formula of recognition from the book of Ezekiel: a word of
judgment directed against the people, a statement concerning
foreign nations, and a divine discourse within the context of a
vision. In 7:2–4 the nation Israel is spoken against:

> An end has come. The end (has come?) upon the four corners of the
> land. Now the end is upon you, and I will let loose my anger upon
> you, and will judge you according to your ways; and I will punish
> you for all your abominations. And my eye will not spare you, nor
> will I have pity; but I will punish you for your ways, while your
> abominations are in your midst. Then you will know that I am
> Yahweh.

In 25:3–5 the neighboring Ammonites are spoken against:

> Because you said, "Aha!" over my sanctuary when it was profaned,
> and over the land of Israel when it was made desolate, and over the
> house of Judah when it went into exile; therefore I am handing you
> over to the people of the East for a possession, and they shall set
> their encampments among you and make their dwellings in your

> midst; they shall eat your fruit, and they shall drink your milk. I will make Rabbah a pasture for camels and the (cities of the?) Ammonites a fold for flocks. Then you will know that I am Yahweh. (RSV)

Within the context of the great vision of the awakening of the bones we hear Yahweh's words to those bones (37:5 ff.):

> Behold, I will cause (life) spirit to enter you, and you shall live. And I will lay sinews upon you, and will cause flesh to come upon you, and cover you with skin, and put (life) spirit in you, and you shall live; and you shall know that I am Yahweh.

In all three examples the Word of God merges into the statement of recognition as its final constituent part, suggesting that this recognition of Yahweh is the final goal and actual culmination of what is spoken in the preceding divine discourse. This positioning of the formula as the concluding target statement of a larger discursive structure predominates in the book of Ezekiel. In more than half the passages, the formula appears at the end of a clearly delineated discursive sequence, and in a series of other passages it appears at the end of such a sequence within the larger context of the speech. Only in approximately one-fifth of the passages does the speech continue uninterrupted beyond the statement of recognition. This tempts us to conclude that the end position is the formula's normal position, whereas its integration into a larger continuing structure represents a modulation that displaces the strict concluding form.

How can we more closely describe the occurrence that reaches its goal in this recognition of Yahweh? Our three examples now yield a second insight representative of the Ezekiel texts as a whole. The remarks preceding the statement of recognition say nothing about any sort of human effort or intellectual exercise that leads to the goal of recognition of Yahweh, though this is what we might expect from the perspective of the epistemological processes familiar to us. All three examples portray an act of Yahweh immediately preceding the statement of recognition, and Yahweh speaks of this action in the first person. Concerning the formal positioning of the statement of recognition we can thus say that this

statement, in which human beings are the subject of the action, is
always anchored in a textual context in which first Yahweh is the
subject of the action.

Two smaller textual groups do not quite seem to fit into this
scheme. On the one hand we have the representative textual
complex in 12:19 f. in which the Word of God says the following
about the inhabitants of Jerusalem:

> They shall eat their bread with fearfulness, and drink water in
> dismay, because their[15] land will be stripped of all it contains, on
> account of the violence of all those who dwell in it. And the
> inhabited cities shall be laid waste, and the land shall become a
> desolation; and you shall know that I am Yahweh. (RSV)

These words are unique in that they portray the coming disaster
quite impersonally. The context, however, leaves no doubt that this
disaster represents Yahweh's judgment. Other passages show by
their form how the impersonal description emerges from Yahweh's
personal speech. This is the case in 6:3–7:

> Behold, I, even I, will bring a sword upon you, and I will destroy
> your high places. Your altars shall become desolate, and your
> incense altars shall be broken; and I will cast down your slain before
> your idols . . . and I will scatter your bones round about your altars.
> Wherever you dwell your cities shall be waste and your high places
> ruined, so that your altars will be waste and ruined, your idols
> broken and destroyed, your incense altars cut down, and your
> works wiped out. And the slain fall in the midst of you, and you
> shall know that I am Yahweh. (RSV)

Here it is quite clear that even the objective description of coming
disaster portrays that disaster as caused by Yahweh.

In chapter 24, verses 25–27 illustrate the second exception to
our rule. Yahweh announces that a fugitive will come from
Jerusalem; in this context the prophet says: "You shall speak and be
no longer dumb. So you will be a sign to them; and they will know
that I am Yahweh." Even though the statement of recognition
follows the description of human action, the mention of the
symbolic function of the prophetic action already shows that the
prophet does not act independently, either in his silence or in his
speech. His action is rather an aid to the proclamation of Yahweh's

great deed: that is why the divine subject is mentioned in another passage clearly prior to the acting human subject. According to 2:5 the people "will know that there has been a prophet among them" because the prophet will appear with the messenger formula, "thus says the Lord Yahweh."[16] Ezekiel 2:3, however, has already named the divine agent sending the human messenger: "Son of man, I send you to the people of Israel." Chapter 28, verses 25–26 also nicely demonstrate this emergence of what appears to be independent human action out of Yahweh's great deeds and offers a rule for understanding them:

> When I gather the house of Israel from the peoples among whom they are scattered, and manifest my holiness in them in the sight of the nations, then they shall dwell in their own land which I gave to my servant Jacob. And they shall dwell securely in it, and they shall build houses and plant vineyards. They shall dwell securely, when I execute judgments upon all their neighbors who have treated them with contempt. Then they will know that I am Yahweh, their God. (RSV)

The other passages in which human action immediately precedes the statement of recognition can also be understood in the light of this subordination of human action to divine action.[17]

Accordingly, we can assert without qualification that the statement of recognition never appears in an isolated position. Instead, it frequently functions as a conclusion, is firmly anchored in the context of prophetic speech, and is always preceded by a statement concerning a divine act. This can be depicted in a completely neutral fashion in its simple historical occurrence, or it can be depicted in such a way that human participation in this divine occurrence becomes visible. Yahweh, however, is always the author of this previously described action.

This formal observation already discloses a significant objective characteristic of the event of recognition that can be mentioned here. In the book of Ezekiel, the organization of the statements of recognition shows that knowledge of Yahweh is not the emergence of an image that has first become clear in the human interior; neither is it a process of speculative combination nor the result of an analysis of one's own creaturely condition. Knowledge or recognition of Yahweh is rather an event occurring in the face of Yahweh's acts, acts to which the prophet as proclaimer draws one's attention. In this phrase, "Yahweh's act," we must emphasize not only the subject *Yahweh*, but the word *act* as well. According to all the statements in the book of Ezekiel, recognition never comes about in the face of Yahweh's inactive being (described in nominal clauses). Not one of the 78 (or 80) passages under question in the book of Ezekiel offers us a description of Yahweh's essence or being. It is always a matter of Yahweh's intervention, either in the history of the hostile nations or of the people of God themselves.

Two insights into the overall system of the recognition formula allow us to be a bit more precise in our determinations. The formula is normally joined to the description of Yahweh's action in the *perfectum consecutivum* with *w*.[18] At first we consciously limited ourselves to speaking about the attainment of the goal and the culmination of the Word of God in the statements of recognition. Now, however, we must look a bit more closely. How should we interpret this *w* that connects the statement of recognition to the preceding sentences? Is this purely a supplementary *w*? Is a statement added here in a purely narrative fashion to what has already been said about Yahweh's deeds, a statement saying that people will recognize Yahweh?

Ezekiel 20:26 offers another possibility. It contains a word Yahweh speaks concerning Israel: "I defiled them through their very gifts when they offered all their first-born by fire, that I might horrify them (give them over to desolation); I did it so that they might know that I am Yahweh." The awkward formulation of the statement, deviating so strongly from what is normal,[19] suggests that the statement of recognition did not originally belong in this context. We should thus consider this formulation to be a redactor's free interpretation of the usual formulations in the book of Ezekiel. As such, however, it is quite significant. We see quite clearly that the editor who added the statement in 20:26 thought of the concluding statement concerning the occurring recognition of God as a final statement. Yahweh's goal in all his actions should become visible in the statement of recognition. If this is indeed the case, then Yahweh's acts, portrayed in the preceding sentences, become the means by which this recognition is elicited. Thus, behind Yahweh's acts there stands the intention that precisely these acts will bring about knowledge. This interpretation, represented by 20:26, is additionally supported by three passages in which the statement of recognition in Ezekiel is employed with infinitives. All three passages (20:12, 20 add the infinitive with a simple *l*; 38:16 adds it with the fuller *lm'n*)[20] understand the recognition formula as a concluding target statement.

These more specific interpretations show that the normal form also constitutes a target statement that is thrown in to relief, even though the statement of recognition here in the *perfectum consecutivum* seems quite unobtrusively to follow the foregoing *perfecta consecutiva* that depict Yahweh's acts. The final level of intention of the divine acts becomes visible in it. God's acts do not occur for their own sake, but rather are directed at human beings; they mean to influence human beings and to create knowledge in them—and that also means, as we shall later see more clearly, to elicit from them acknowledgement of Yahweh.[21] Yahweh acts because he wants to effect this acknowledgement among human beings.

Our translations must also reflect the fact that the statement of recognition in the divine view must always resonate something of a concluding finality. From the human viewpoint this finality emerges as a secondary accent with quietly imperative overtones. The purely indicative translation of the statement of recognition in the prophetic word, "(I will act), and they *shall* know that I am Yahweh," clearly emphasizes the accent of sovereign divine machinations that in the final analysis also elicit recognition in human beings. In addition, however, we need to consider the translation, "(I will act), and they *should* recognize that I am Yahweh." This allows the imperative that confronts human beings to resonate in their freedom of decision and calls them to obedience. In a fundamental sense, of course, both elements are always contained in the prophetic pronouncement, and it is not always easy to determine which of the two accents emerge more strongly in any given instance.

Considering this insight into the structure of the divine Word, we can now easily understand a second finding concerning the

formal extension of the entire textual complex. In 25:16–17 we hear
a divine statement directed against the Philistines:

> Behold, I will stretch out my hand against the Philistines, and I will cut
> off the Cherethites, and destroy the rest [of the inhabitants of] the
> seacoast. I will execute great vengeance upon them with wrathful
> chastisements. Then they will [should] know that I am Yahweh, when
> I lay my vengeance upon them [btty 't nqmty bm]. (RSV)

It is obvious that the divine statement does not end with the statement
of recognition as it did in the other statements concerning foreign
nations (25:5, 7, 11; 26:6). Rather, the statement of recognition is
again followed by a statement summarizing the preceding description
of the divine acts: "when I lay my vengeance upon them." This
supplemental clause, consisting of a suffixed infinitive joined by *b*,
summarizes for the second time the content of the divine action and
shows that precisely Yahweh's action is the basis for the targeted
recognition. Indeed, beyond that one can even say comprehensively
that it is the "material" for that recognition. This clearly discloses the
juxtaposition of human recognition to divine action.[22]

In 30:8 we see that this supplementary clause, a clause
summarizing something already said, can also demonstrate a
tendency toward extension itself. Here an extension in the
perfectum consecutivum is added to the infinitive expression, and
thus the discourse returns to the form in which the prophetic word
preceding the statement of recognition had already described
Yahweh's acts, acts themselves preceding any recognition of
Yahweh. "Then they will know that I am Yahweh, when I have set
fire to Egypt, and all her helpers are broken [btty . . . wnšbrw]."
Passages such as 6:13; 12:15; 15:7; 20:42, 44; 28:22; 39:28 show that
this kind of extension can continue even further. However, the most
sonorous conclusion of a discourse occurs when the extension
commencing with *b* and an infinitive is concluded a second time with
the recognition formula. This is the case in the conclusion to
30:20–26; beginning with verse 22 the threat reads:

> Behold, I am against Pharaoh king of Egypt, and will break his arms
> . . . I will strengthen the arms of the king of Babylon . . . but the
> arms of Pharaoh shall fall; and they shall know that I am Yahweh,
> when I put my sword into the hand of the king of Babylon [btty] and

he stretches it out against the land of Egypt; and I will scatter the Egyptians among the nations and disperse them throughout the countries. Then they will [should] know that I am Yahweh. (RSV)

In 34:27–30 and 37:13–14 the same full, concluding doubling of the statement of recognition is demonstrated.[23]

From this perspective we can draw a conclusion concerning the translation of these passages analogous to the one drawn concerning the translation of the *perfectum consecutivum* of the statement of recognition. The *b* introducing the following (or preceding, see below) infinitive is apparently not fully understood if taken only temporally. The translation of 24:24, "When [then, whenever] this comes, you will know that I am the Lord Yahweh," does not yet do full justice to the content of the Hebraic statement *bb'h*. The instrumental secondary meaning of *b* must be made audible: "In the fact that this comes you will know that I am the Lord Yahweh." The infinitive clause introduced by *b* mentions not only the moment of the advent of recognition, but also the conditions igniting that recognition, its cause. Besides the passage cited, 24:24, this infinitive statement introduced by *b* is also placed before the statement of recognition in 32:15 and 33:33, though normally the infinitive follows it.[24] In any case, before translating it one must first consider where the accents lie in each given instance. Here, too, both emphases can almost be discerned.

In all these substantive determinations of content we have almost gotten too far ahead of ourselves, since we are actually still dealing with the question concerning the formal uniqueness and origin of the recognition formula. It is time to expand our overview of the material in Ezekiel to include the context of the Old Testament at large. Can we find something there of this formula that so strikingly characterizes the book of Ezekiel? Or is it actually characteristic only of Ezekiel?[25]

3. The Statement of Recognition in the Rest of the Old Testament

(a) *1 Kings 20*

I Kings 20 tells of the Syrian wars of King Ahab of Israel and is a narrative probably originating in the circles of the national-Israelite prophetic group. It is characteristic of this group that prophetic figures appear at crucial times and either influence events through the Word of God they proclaim or pass judgment on them from the perspective of that word. The criteria of this word of judgment are Yahweh's honor and his strict demand for the ban, a concept originating in the motif of the holy war (20:13–14, 22, 28, 35–43). By trying to separate out the brief comments concerning the intervention of the prophets, Eissfeldt removes the very heart of the account, and Noth has quite justifiably rejected this operation.[26] Two of the prophetic speeches found in this chapter are of particular significance for our study.

When Ahab, besieged in the city of Samaria, rejects a dishonorable capitulation to the boasting Syrian king and prepares his defenses in the war of the first year, a prophet comes and addresses him: "Thus says Yahweh, Have you seen all this great multitude? Behold, I will give it into your hand this day; and you shall know that I am Yahweh" (20:13, rsv). The same thing happens in the war of the following year, during which Syria fights against the Israelites on the plain because word circulated after the previous year's defeat that Yahweh was a god of the hills. Before the beginning of the battle a man of God again comes to the king and says: "Thus says Yahweh, 'Because the Syrians have said, "Yahweh is a god of the hills but he is not a god of the valleys," therefore I will give all this great multitude into your hand, and you shall know that I am Yahweh' " (20:28, rsv).

In both these prophetic speeches in extremely pure and terse form, we surprisingly encounter the same kind of prophetic speech merging into the statement of recognition that was so characteristic of the book of Ezekiel. At the center of both sayings stands the prediction of Yahweh's intervention into the present situation ("I will give them over into your hand"), and in both cases a legitimation precedes this announcement. In verse 13 we hear the understated question, "Have you seen all this great multitude?" One still hears the echo of the Syrian king's words boasting of his power: "The gods do so to me, and more also, if the dust of Samaria shall suffice for handfuls for all the people who follow me" (20:10, rsv). Verse 28 tersely formulates the legitimation: "Because the

Syrians have said . . . therefore . . . ." In both examples the now-familiar statement of recognition follows in its most strict formulation, as *perfectum consecutivum* introduced by *w* and void of any supplementary additions. As was the rule in the book of Ezekiel, the statement of recognition stands at the conclusion and designates the actual goal of Yahweh's intervention, namely, the event of recognition.[27] The content of both divine speeches in 1 Kings 20 is the prediction of a divine act in which Yahweh, in the face of his people's enemies, shows himself through this granting of victory to be Israel's true God.

The two prophetic discourses in 1 Kings 20 cannot be dependent on the book of Ezekiel. In the almost classic terseness of their diction, in the unaffected way they express a national-Israelite salvation theology in the northern Israel sphere—a theology showing them to be influenced by the concept of the holy war[28]—they represent a completely independent, older formulation. The account in 1 Kings 20 leads us back into the middle of the ninth century and was probably committed to writing at or shortly after the same time. It contains a great many details concerning the individual phases of the Syrian wars and still lets us sense the agitation certain political decisions of the king of Israel (the release of Ben-hadad) precipitated in prophetic circles. In addition, Ahab's image has not yet been colored by the totally hostile views of the Elijah legend and later tradition. One should by no means try to date it after the end of the Northern Kingdom.[29]

Thus, we stand before the significant conclusion that the book of Ezekiel, with its profuse use of the statement of recognition, is a relatively late witness to a significantly older tradition of prophetic discourse structure, a tradition already manifested in the prophetic groups of the Northern Kingdom. That which in the book of Ezekiel is so quickly noticeable and appears to be one of its characteristic elements is by no means an original coinage of Ezekiel himself. This prophet stands rather, along with the circle that edited his book, within a specific prophetic tradition surrounding this particular form of the prophetic saying, a tradition going back certainly two and perhaps even three centuries.

Can we follow this tradition of divine discourse formulation back even further? If so, then the Moses tradition will be of particular significance.

(b) *The Moses Tradition*

Nowhere in Old Testament narrative does the recognition formula in both its strict as well as its freely altered form appear in such profusion as in the accounts of Moses' deeds.

It may not seem particularly significant for the evaluation of the formulation's prehistory that this assertion happens to be based on the accounts of the *Priestly Writing*. After all, this writing was very likely composed only in the postexilic period, and this fact would prompt us to see in it only part of the subsequent history of the linguistic usage we saw in Ezekiel. Indeed, several factors suggest that Ezekiel had some sort of relationship to the Priestly circles (living in Babylon) that stand behind the Priestly Writing. Nevertheless, the questions still remain: why did the Priestly writers feel that this stylization after the model of Ezekiel's prophetic speeches was so necessary only here in the story of Moses, and why did they employ it there in so penetrating a fashion? Why do none of the divine discourses in Genesis employ the recognition formula? This question takes on quite different features, however, when we find that even the Moses story in the older narrative writings shows this peculiar employment of the recognition formula, though on the whole they use the recognition formula in a more varied fashion. This suggests that even the Priestly Writing, in its own versions of the Moses story, is not to be understood only from the perspective of its proximity to Ezekiel. Rather, it stands quite firmly in the force field of the older Moses tradition and is thus itself a branch of tradition that is independent of Ezekiel. For this reason it warrants particular attention in the context of our discussion.

In the Priestly Moses tradition the statement of recognition occurs first in Exodus 6:7 in the context of Yahweh's great revelatory speech to Moses.[30] After revealing himself in his name "Yahweh," Yahweh commissions Moses to speak to the people. As Yahweh's spokesman, Moses is to announce Yahweh's incipient deeds to them:

> I will bring you out from under the burdens of the Egyptians, and I will deliver you from their bondage, and I will redeem you with an outstretched arm and with great acts of judgment, and I will take you for my people, and I will be your God; and you shall know that I am Yahweh, your God, who has brought you out . . . and I will bring you into the land . . . (6:6–9, RSV)

The end position of the formula has been obscured here. Yahweh's saving deed is described anew in the form of a participial extension of the kind we saw in Ezekiel, an extension that then passes unnoticed into the finite verbal form characteristic of the hymnic style (here the *perfectum consecutivum*).

Exodus 7:5, where the statement of recognition comes from Yahweh himself, also contains the kind of infinitival repetition of an announcement of divine action that we have already seen in Ezekiel. After Yahweh has announced his impending deed to Moses, verse 5 concludes the divine discourse that began in 7:1: "And the Egyptians shall know that I am Yahweh, when I [*bntty,* by the fact that I] stretch forth my hand upon Egypt and bring out the people of Israel from among them" (RSV).

In Exodus 14, the Priestly account of the crossing of the sea, two strikingly similar Yahweh speeches appear with the statement of recognition (vss. 4, 17 f.). The second speech, in verse 18, also uses repetition: "And the Egyptians shall know that I am Yahweh, when I (by the fact that I, *bhkbdy*) have gotten glory over Pharaoh, his chariots, and his horsemen" (RSV). The entire situation surrounding both passages in Exodus recalls the prophetic speeches in 1 Kings 20. Just as was the case during the struggles with the Syrians, so also does a divine speech here announce help in an hour of (Egyptian) enemy threat.

The Priestly manna narrative in Exodus 16 also employs a doubling of the statement of recognition. The source question in this chapter is extremely difficult to answer, though we can hardly doubt that the two verses of significance for our study are Priestly. In 16:6 we hear Moses' and Aaron's answer to the people's murmuring about being taken away from the fleshpots of Egypt: "At evening you shall know that it was Yahweh who brought you out of the land of Egypt, and in the morning you shall see the glory of Yahweh, when [because, in the fact that *bšm'w*] he has heard [answered] your murmurings. . . .''[31] Moses' words announce a sign that will confirm the truth of the entire Exodus event. Shortly thereafter, the people are called "before Yahweh" (before the tent, which in that case would appear here somewhat prematurely?). Moses now speaks in the perfect tense of the statement of recognition: "Come near before Yahweh, for he has heard [answered] your murmurings" (16:9, RSV). Yahweh himself, however, appearing in his glory in a cloud, commissions Moses to announce the actual words of answer and the confirming sign: "Say to them, 'At twilight you shall eat flesh, and in the morning you shall be filled with bread; then you shall know that I am Yahweh, your God' " (16:12 RSV). There then follows the distribution of quails and manna in the evening and morning.

One cannot fail to see the conceptually delineated, theologically reflected context of the statements in which the Priestly Writing employs the statement of recognition. Exodus 14 speaks of Yahweh's show of power before the Egyptians as his self-glorification (*hkbd*), through which he made himself recognizable. In Exodus 16 we first hear it in Moses' announcement that Israel will see Yahweh's glory. Shortly thereafter Yahweh's glory is visible to the entire people. Yahweh himself expresses the content of this knowledge in the slightly extended, though strict formula: "Know, that I am Yahweh, your God." In Moses' preliminary announcement this content was appropriately developed: "Know, that Yahweh brought [you] out of the land of Egypt." In this sense to know Yahweh does not mean to encounter some part of Yahweh's transcendent being, but rather to recognize his beneficial deed on Israel's behalf. Yahweh's fundamental beneficial deed on Israel's behalf, however, is the leading out of Egypt. It is no accident that this act already completely dominates the statements in Exodus 6:7 and 7:5.

It also dominates the next Priestly passage in which the recognition formula appears. At the end of the statutes concerning the tent of meeting (Exod. 30 f. contain addenda) and related matters, Yahweh's activity as announced to Israel is now summarized:

> I will meet with the people of Israel, and I will show myself holy in
> my glory . . . and will dwell among the people of Israel, and will be
> their God. And they shall know that I am Yahweh, their God, who
> brought them forth out of the land of Egypt that I might dwell
> among them; I am Yahweh, their God. (Exod. 29:43–46)[32]

According to the addendum in Exodus 31:12–17, one part of
the covenant between Yahweh and Israel is the sabbath. In all the
generations of Israel it is to be kept as a sign between Yahweh and
Israel, ". . . that you may know that I, Yahweh, sanctify you." This
formulation is similar to the statement in Ezekiel 20:12. We will
have to deal with it again in a later context[33] because Yahweh is to be
known as the God sanctifying Israel not by his direct action, but
rather—in a deviation from what we have previously seen—by
means of a sign Israel is to keep.

Two additional, more freely formulated passages can conclude
our look at the Priestly Writing. Leviticus 23:43 is a variation of the
assertion that Yahweh is to be known by his deed of leading the
people out of Egypt. The instruction to live in booths during the
thanksgiving feast is concluded with the remark: ". . . that your
generations may know [lm'n yēḏ'û drtykm], that I made the people
of Israel dwell in booths when I brought them out of the land of
Egypt: I am Yahweh, your God."[34] As was the case with the sabbath
commandment, the keeping of a festival ordinance is mentioned as
a means of knowing Yahweh through his special acts on Israel's
behalf. As regards the passage in Numbers 14:34, one is not really
sure whether to mention it at all here. The people, who are
disobedient in the face of the spys' reports, are told that they must
remain forty years in the desert "so that you shall know my
resistance (displeasure?)." We can in any case clearly see here that
the Priestly Writing, too, was familiar with the sometimes
dangerous, judging character of Yahweh's acts on behalf of his
people.

Our overview shows that most of the Priestly passages employ
the same strict formulation of the statement of recognition that we
encountered in Ezekiel. They are integrated into a theologically
sophisticated context in which Yahweh's initial deed on Israel's
behalf—the leading out of Egypt mentioned in Israel's credo—plays

a central role. It can be called both the means to knowledge as well as the actual content of knowledge (Exod. 6:7; 16:6).

The picture changes somewhat when we examine the *older source-texts of the Moses tradition.*

Instead of the *perfectum consecutivum* of *yd'* connected with *w*, we usually find at the beginning of the statement of recognition the express final particle (*lm'n* 8:6, 18; 9:29; 11:7; and in the secondary addendum in 9:14 once as *b'bwr*) followed by the imperfect. Instead of the strict formulation, "know that I am Yahweh," we also find as knowledge-content more freely altered statements concerning Yahweh's superiority and his elective action on Israel's behalf. The statement's theological terseness as we saw it in P is missing here.

Of the three passages in which we encounter the strict formula outside of P, Exodus 10:1–2 belongs in the context of a later textual addition. Yahweh speaks:

> I have hardened his (Pharaoh's) heart and the heart of his servants, that I may show these signs of mine among them (let them occur among them), and that you may tell in the hearing of your son and your son's son how I have made sport of the Egyptians and what signs I have done among them; that you may know that I am Yahweh.

Again we hear of signs that Yahweh has performed and of which more will be said later; knowledge of Yahweh should emerge from this subsequent telling.

Exodus 8:20 leads us into what is probably the Yahwistic context of the prediction of the plague of flies. Under Yahweh's commission, Moses speaks to the Pharaoh: "But on that day I will set apart the land of Goshen, where my people dwell, so that no swarms of flies shall be there; that you may know that I am Yahweh in the midst of the earth." Verse 23 calls this divine act a sign: "Thus I will put a division between my people and your people. By tomorrow shall this sign be" (RSV).

The third passage containing the strict formula probably also belongs to J, and it prompts us to make two formal observations. First, in 7:17 we encounter yet a third way of relating the statement of Yahweh's action to the statement of recognition; the words directed to Pharaoh are: "By this you shall know [*bz't td'*] that I ['ny] am Yahweh: behold, I ['nky] strike the water that is in the Nile with the rod that is in my hand . . ." (RSV). We have already seen the normal form (statement of recognition in the end position) and the possibility of a summarizing repetition of the statement of God's action that thus frames the statement of recognition both in front and behind. This third possibility shows that the statement of recognition can stand at the beginning of the textual complex. The statement about Yahweh's action, normally standing in the first position, has been reduced to the brief pronominal expression *bz't* (by this you shall know); the execution of this act has been placed entirely after the statement of recognition. This emphatic positioning of the statement of recognition at the beginning boldly underscores the significance of the knowledge to be gained in the encounter with this divine act. It confirms once again what we found in our analysis of the passages in Ezekiel, namely, that knowledge of Yahweh is not some incidental occurrence on the fringe of the other statements about Yahweh's acts. It is rather the actual goal of those actions. Yahweh's deeds whether among Pharaoh and the Egyptians or the Israelites, attain their goal wherever they bring about knowledge of Yahweh; a peculiar solidarity exists here between both friends and enemies of Yahweh.

A second striking observation is that in 7:17 the form *'ny* and the form *'nky* of the personal pronoun in the first person singular occur in immediate succession. A comparison with related passages (7:27; 8:24, 25; cf. however also 9:27 and 11:4) suggests that the narrator prefers *'nky* in his own formulation. Should we conclude from this appearance of *'ny* in the statement of recognition that J was already familiar with a formulaic employment of the statement?[35]

Instances of a more freely formulated statement of recognition occur more frequently in the older textual sources. In Exodus 8:9 Moses gives to Pharaoh himself the opportunity to determine when the plague of frogs should end. Again we clearly discern the idea of a proof-sign. Pharaoh's wish is that the plague end on the following day; to this Moses answers, "Be it as you say, that you may know that there is no one like Yahweh, our God" (RSV). The situation is similar in 9:29; Pharaoh entreats for an end to the hail, and Moses answers, "As soon as I have gone out of the city, I will stretch out my hands to Yahweh: the thunder will cease, and there be no more hail, that you may know that the earth is Yahweh's" (RSV). And again in 11:7, after he threatens Pharaoh with the death of all first born, Moses says, "But against any of the people of Israel, either man or beast, not a dog shall growl; that you may know that Yahweh makes a distinction between the Egyptians and Israel" (RSV). This statement no doubt also refers to knowledge of Yahweh; again, however, this does not mean knowledge of some transcendent, self-contained essence of Yahweh. Rather it comes about in a completely concrete fashion so that the Egyptians, as in 8:20 f. above, recognize something of the distinction between Egypt and Israel, between those who are the people of God and those who are not. Conceptually this statement is similar to the Priestly statement in the story of the spies, according to which the punishment of the generation in the desert shows what Yahweh's resistance, his no, means. Thus Yahweh deals with the Egyptians in such a way that every person can recognize the distinction between Yahweh's yes and his no. Yahweh is known by his dealings with human beings either in election or punishment.

We must also mention Exodus 9:14, to which belongs the secondary addendum 9:14–16. Moses again speaks to Pharaoh, "For this time I will send all my plagues upon your heart, and upon your servants and your people, that you may know [*b'bwr td'*] that there is none like me in all the earth" (RSV). We should note the merging of the entire insertion with verse 16. Pharaoh is told: "But for this purpose have I let you live, to show you my power, so that my name may be declared throughout all the earth" (RSV). This transcends even what we saw in 10:2. The truth that Yahweh's actions bring to Pharaoh should by this very event be extended beyond these specific circumstances so that Pharaoh's knowledge becomes knowledge for all the world. The recognition of Yahweh should take place not only among his own people, but among the hostile peoples as well.

Within the framework of the Moses story in the older sources we certainly cannot pass over Moses' speech in numbers 16:28–30, which leads us to the dramatic climax of Moses' encounter with

Dathan and Abiram.[36] Moses himself goes to the tents of the mutinous group around Dathan and Abiram, who will not answer his summons. They stand before their tents, and in the face of the assembled congregation, whom Moses has told to depart from the tents, he says:

> Hereby [bz't] you shall know that Yahweh has sent me to do all these works, and that it has not been of my own accord. If these men die the common death of all men, and are (only) visited by the fate of all men (namely, a peaceful death in old age), then Yahweh has not sent me. But if Yahweh performs a miracle [bry'h ybr', literally: creates something new], and the ground opens its mouth, and swallows them up, with all that belongs to them, and they go down alive into Sheol, then you shall know that these men have despised Yahweh.

Our first observation is that we find here a particularly rich amplification of the elements of the formal integration of the statement of recognition. The entire discourse lands by the statement of recognition with the *perfectum consecutivum* in the fashion we saw favored in Ezekiel. However, because of the significance of the target recognition, the recognition that in actuality resolves the tense situation, the possibility of an emphatic anticipation of the statement of recognition is combined with it by a short, preliminary *bz't* ("hereby you shall know"). The discourse is thus completely framed by both an introductory and a concluding statement of recognition. The discourse's announcement of Yahweh's action leads one to expect a sign that has been heightened to the full force of the divine judgment of condemnation. Verses 31 ff. then tell of its immediate occurrence.

However, can we justifiably consider this passage together with those statements that speak of a recognition of Yahweh? The introductory statement of recognition tells us that the content of that knowledge here is that "you shall know that Yahweh has sent me." Is this not something different than what is so clearly expressed in the strict formulation, "know that I am Yahweh"? The concluding formulation summarizes in the following fashion the intention of the story: "You shall know that these men have despised Yahweh." This suggests that the recognition or lack of recognition of Moses' commission is nothing more than the recognition or lack of recognition of Yahweh. In both cases we are virtually coerced into replacing the word "recognition" by the word "acknowledgment." This clearly shows once again that the strict recognition formula is apparently never really concerned with Yahweh's self-contained being, but rather with his coming self-manifestation and demand for obedience. This is the only way we can understand how the formula can covertly incorporate into itself the recognition and acknowledgment of the divine mouthpiece as well. Under certain circumstances, this recognition and acknowledgment also decides the recognition and acknowledgment of Yahweh. It is impossible to overlook the suggestion in Numbers 16 that to reject Moses' commission is to despise Yahweh. The recognition process for the sake of which Moses calls forth the divine judgment encompasses both the acknowledgment of Yahweh as Lord and the acknowledgment that speaks for Yahweh.

Let us summarize retrospectively what this examination of the older Moses tradition has revealed. We observe first, of course, that here we have found the recognition formula richly employed. The distribution in these older texts is particularly concentrated in the accounts of the signs and plagues preceding the departure from Egypt. The texts emphasize again and again that these unusual occurrences are transparent for the sake of a certain piece of knowledge. Indeed, we can formulate this more correctly by avoiding this static statement and saying rather: the purpose of the great signs is to prompt recognition of Yahweh in Israel, in the Pharaoh, and beyond them in all the world. The frequent addition of the statement of recognition with the particle *lm'n* clearly shows that this recognition is not some incidental, secondary product of Yahweh's acts, but is *the* goal Yahweh actually intends.

We found the strict recognition formula most frequently in the theologically more sophisticated Priestly Writing, although it was not completely absent in the older accounts. On the whole, however, the older accounts tended to alter and modify the formulation's content (the knowledge itself) more freely and richly. Numbers 16 showed in addition that the recognition (acknowledgment) of Yahweh could also include the recognition (acknowledgment) of his emissary. If we can legitimately assign the pre-Priestly statements in the Moses tradition to J, then this also enables us to follow the tradition of the strict statement of recognition beyond 1 Kings 20 back into the early period of kings. Even that early period employed the recognition formula as a form of speech from Yahweh himself or from his earthly emissary. In contrast to Ezekiel and to 1 Kings 20, however, we find the formula here outside of what is in the strict sense prophetic literature, and this prevents us from designating this literary device as an exclusively prophetic form. It seems to have been at home in a variety of circumstances from the very beginning.

We still need to consider the *Deuteronomic portion of the Moses tradition and the Deuteronomistic statements in general.*

At least according to its structure, the strict recognition formula is part of Yahweh's personal speech or of that of the person authorized to speak under the auspices of the divine first person. Deuteronomy, however, is stylized as Moses' paraenetical exposition of the Law;[37] hence from the very beginning one would not expect to find the strict statement of recognition in Deuteronomy. A statement such as that in Deuteronomy 29:4 f. sounds strangely awkward and is most likely a secondary insertion; in a retrospective view of the desert period Moses says the following in the middle of one of his speeches: "I have led you forty years in the wilderness . . . you have not eaten bread, and you have not drunk wine or strong drink; that you may know [*lm'n td'w*] that I am Yahweh."

Nevertheless, the more freely formulated statement of recognition is not completely absent in Deuteronomy. First, it can appear in appropriately expanded form within the context of a paraenetical historical retrospect, as in 4:32 ff.. Again within the context of the signs and miracles associated with the departure from Egypt we hear:

> For ask now of the days that are past. . . . Did any people ever hear the voice of a god speaking out of the midst of a fire? . . . Or has any god ever attempted to go and take a nation for himself from the midst of another nation, by trials, by signs, by wonders, and by war, by a mighty hand and an outstretched arm, and by great terrors, according to all that Yahweh, your God, did for you in Egypt before

your eyes? To you it was shown, that you might know [*ld't*] that
Yahweh is God; there is no other besides him. (RSV)

In 7:6, 8*b*, 9[38] the reference to Yahweh's elective action on
Israel's behalf similarly takes the following form:

> . . . and [he] redeemed you from the house of bondage, from the
> hand of Pharaoh king of Egypt. Know therefore [*wyd't*] that
> Yahweh, your God is God, the faithful God who keeps covenant
> and steadfast love with those who love him and keep his
> commandments, to a thousand generations. (RSV)

Here we encounter once again the normal form of expansion in the
perfectum consecutivum. The paraenetical context of this whole
exposition only permits the translation, "know therefore." The
imperative component of the statement of recognition, a component we have seen in Ezekiel, is clearly recognizable here.

This is particularly clear in the paraenetically divided,
extended formulation in 4:39. The reference to Yahweh's great
deed is followed by the open paraenesis still given here formally in
the *perfectum consecutivum*:[39] "Know therefore this day, and lay it
to your heart, that Yahweh is God in heaven above and on the earth
beneath; there is no other. Therefore you shall keep his statutes and
his commandments . . . " (RSV). Recognition here includes keeping
the commandments.

The formulation, "know that Yahweh is God" (*ky yhwh hw'
h'lhym*),[40] is apparently the specific Deuteronomic designation of
the content of the knowledge. Indeed, we also find it in the narrative
literature that is dependent on Deuteronomy. In 1 Kings 8:60 it is
part of a prayer. Solomon prays that Yahweh may do justice to the
king and the people "that all the peoples of the earth may know
[*lm'n d't*] that Yahweh is God; there is no other" (RSV). Hezekiah's
prayer uses the same formulation when he is pressed by Assyrian
demands for capitulation: "Save us from his hand, that all the
kingdoms of the earth may know [*w'yēd' û*] that thou, Yahweh, art
God alone" (2 Kings 19:19; shortened in the parallel passage Isa.
37:20).[41] In 2 Chronicles 33:13, on the other hand, the formula has
been revised into narrative. We are told that when Yahweh heard
Manasseh's prayer, "then Manasseh knew that Yahweh was God."

The imperative formulation in Psalm 100:3, "Know that Yahweh is God!" also belongs in this context. On the other hand, we hear in Solomon's prayer of dedication the Deuteronomic reference to the name of Yahweh that dwells in the Temple. Solomon asks that even a foreigner be heard when he calls to Yahweh in this house,

> . . . in order that all the peoples of the earth may know thy name [*lnfn yd'wn*] and fear thee, as do thy people Israel, and that they may know [*wld't*] that this house which I have built is called by thy name. (1 Kings 8:43; par. 2 Chron. 6:33, RSV)

According to Deuteronomic theology, recognition of the presence of Yahweh's name at his elected earthly location is also part of genuine recognition of the Yahweh who acts in history.

In summary, we can say that the occasional employment of the statement of recognition in the Deuteronomic and Deuteronomistic[42] writings does not contribute anything essential to the question of this literary form's origin and original setting. The Deuteronomic passages are of interest only in relation to the subsequent history and secondary employment of the formula. They show that the statement of recognition can pick up and express specifically Deuteronomic concerns (Yahweh's exclusivity, revelation in his name at a specific locale). The imperative component in the statement of recognition also necessarily leads us only into a certain proximity to Deuteronomy's overall paraenetic atmosphere. Perhaps Deuteronomy's main contribution to the history of the recognition formula lies in this paraenetic development of the statement of recognition. Deuteronomy 4:39 f. suggests that to recognize Yahweh means to "lay it to your heart" (*hšyb 'l lbb*)[43] and that recognition prompts one to keep Yahweh's statutes and commandments. 1 Kings 8:43 says that the recognition of Yahweh's name leads to fear of Yahweh. It is put very clearly here that recognition of Yahweh means obedience to Yahweh.

(c) *Deutero-Isaiah*

In Deutero-Isaiah the recognition formula, both in its strict as well as in its expanded form, plays a significant role. Close

observation reveals that this turn of phrase occurs in two
characteristically different forms of prophetic discourse.

It was Begrich who disclosed that Deutero-Isaiah often clothed
his message in the form of the priestly supplication oracle.[44] Three
passages in which we encounter the strict form of the statement of
recognition in Deutero-Isaiah point to its employment in this way.
We hear it first within the framework of the great oracular
statement to Cyrus. Here, too, the statement of recognition at the
conclusion of the first strophe is preceded by statements concerning
Yahweh's acts. "I will go before you . . . I will give you treasures of
darkness and the hoards in secret places, that you may know [lm'n
td'] that it is I, Yahweh, the God of Israel, who call you by your
name" (45:2 f., RSV). "I call you by your name . . . I am Yahweh
. . . I gird you . . . that men may know [lm'n yēḏ'û] from the rising of
the sun and from the west, that there is none besides me; I am
Yahweh, and there is no other" (45:4–6, RSV).[45] To this we add the
two supplication answers in 49:22–26. In the first Yahweh
announces to those of his people who are dispersed among the
nations that they will return to their land. The statement concludes:
"Then you will know [or: know therefore] that I am Yahweh; those
who wait for me shall not be put to shame" (49:23, RSV). The second
passage promises Yahweh's victory over the enemies of his people
and designates the following as the goal of this action: "Then all
flesh shall know that I am Yahweh, your Savior, and your
Redeemer, the Mighty One of Jacob" (49:26, RSV; subsequently,
60:16). The noticeably awkward formulation in 52:6, "Therefore
my people shall know my name; there in that day, [they shall
know?] that it is I who speak; here am I," echoes the recognition
formula slightly, but is likely a secondary addedum. At the
conclusion to the supplication answer in 41:17–20 we hear the
recognition formula extended in a fashion recalling the paraenetic
expansiveness of Deuteronomy. This passage portrays the miraculous leading of the people through the desert, "that [lm'n] men may
see and know, may consider and understand together, that the hand
of Yahweh has done this, the Holy One of Israel has created it"
(RSV).

The other passage in which we hear the recognition formula is one of Deutero-Isaiah's judgment discourses. We hear it in the sharp polemic against idols:

> You [Israel] are my witnesses, says Yahweh,
>   and my servant whom I have chosen,
> that you may know and believe me
>   and understand that I am He [ky'ny hw'].[46]
> Before me no god was formed,
>   nor shall there be any after me.
> I, I am Yahweh,
>   and besides me there is no savior.
> I declared [it] . . . .   (43:10–12, rsv)

Chapter 41, verse 23, in a polemical alteration of the statement of recognition, openly challenges the other gods: "Tell us what is come hereafter, that we may know [wnd'h] that you are gods" (rsv). We hear a strongly forensic element both here and in 41:26; "Who declared it from the beginning, that we might know, and beforetime, that we might say, 'He is right'?" Here recognition also includes something of the judgmental decision in the face of the acts of Yahweh and the other gods. This is not merely a matter of incidental knowledge beneath or beside other knowledge, but rather of the decision concerning the validity or invalidity of dominion.

Deutero-Isaiah is a prophet of the generation after Ezekiel. We might suspect that in his profuse employment of the recognition formula he was influenced by Ezekiel; perhaps he shows us a somewhat later manifestation of the tradition that leads from 1 Kings 20, through what are for us invisible channels, to Ezekiel. Only very superficial observation, however, can support this hypothesis. In reality, our overview of Deutero-Isaiah has strikingly revealed that this prophet's use of the statement of recognition, in contrast to that of 1 Kings 20 and Ezekiel, does not appear in the context of specifically prophetic literary forms (invective, reprimand); indeed, in Deutero-Isaiah prophetic speech forms in general recede to an astonishing degree. Rather, the strict statement of recognition here occurs in the supplication answers, while the more freely altered forms are found in the judgment discourses. These forms are quite different from the prophetic sayings in 1 Kings 20 and Ezekiel. Deutero-Isaiah must then be the product of a line of tradition different from the prophetic traditions we have already seen. Begrich suggests that the statement of recognition was originally at home in the priestly oracular supplication answer, where it was to announce the goal Yahweh was pursuing with that answer; this hypothesis is very persuasive. This means, however, that the conclusion we drew from the Moses stories is confirmed anew from a different perspective. The recognition formula, which in 1 Kings 20 and Ezekiel appears so clearly integrated into a specific type of prophetic speech, can now no longer be limited to this sphere. Its association with the prophetic sayings represents only part of its history; originally it must have been an independent element that entered into combinations other than that. We will have to watch for further examples of this.

On the other hand, the somewhat more indefinite use of the formula in the Deutero-Isian judgment discourses makes it clear that the formula has a certain affinity for forensic events and judgment decisions. Here the statement of recognition apparently does not intend to speak of some mysteriously emerging insight and one's intuitive comprehension of it, but rather of knowledge as the recognition of clear, alternative choices that reflect something of the clarity of legal decisions. Here, too, we need to ask whether this affinity can be understood from the perspective of the formula's original setting.

(d) *The Remaining Old Testament Passages in Which the State-*
    ment of Recognition Is Encountered in Its Strict Formulation

We can quickly enumerate these passages. In the book of Joel we encounter the statement of recognition twice in formulations belonging to the posthistory of the Isaian and Deutero-Isaian manner of speech. Joel 2:27 concludes a discourse that portrays in profuse imagery Yahweh's concluding salvation deed on behalf of his people and his land. All these miraculous events will occur, and

> You shall know that I am in the midst of Israel,
>   and that I, Yahweh, am your God and there is none else.
> And my people shall never again be put to shame.

This broad extension of the statement of recognition recalls Deutero-Isaiah. Beyond this, we can hear an echo of statements such as Isaiah 45:5, 6, 18, 21, 22, or 49:23. The turn of phrase in 3:17, on the other hand, is more strongly proto-Isaian:

> So you shall know that I am Yahweh, your God, [mtr. cs. dl.?]
>   who dwell in Zion, my holy mountian.
> And Jerusalem shall be holy
>   and strangers shall never again pass though it. (RSV)

It is uncertain whether the text in Malachi 2:4 should be read with part of the Greek tradition in a threat against the priests: "(Behold, I cut off your arms, [c. t.]) So shall you know that I have sent this command to you. . . ." If this extension is legitimate, then once again the (verbally expanded) strict formula occurs within the framework of a threat.

The statement of recognition in Psalm 46 is unique for several reasons. It is the only occurrence of the strict formula in which '*ny* is replaced by '*nky*. Verse 11, which openly expresses the latent imperative component in the statement of recognition, is related to the Deuteronomically influenced statement in Psalm 100:3 (cf. also Ps. 4:3). For the rest, however, this psalm's placement of the statement of recognition again recalls the basic structural lines we have seen elsewhere. Here, too, the call to recognition stands at the conclusion.[47] Immediately preceding it is a portrayal of the great and victorious deeds of Yahweh, who directs wars to the end of the earth, breaks the bow, shatters the spear, and burns the chariots with fire. We are in the sphere of holy war, portrayed here on a worldwide scale. In view of Yahweh's deeds, an imperious royal statement demands the putting away of all self-will and the recognition of Yahweh's majesty.

> Be still, and know that I am Yahweh.
>   I am exalted among the nations,
>   I am exalted in the earth. (46:10)

The recognition event is interpreted here in the most decisive fashion as a turning away from, a putting away of human self-will.

Finally, the statement in Jeremiah 24:7 deserves particular attention. We hear Yahweh's promise concerning the exiles of 598:

"I will give them a heart to know me, that I am Yahweh [*ld't'wty ky 'ny yhwh*]; and they shall be my people and I will be their God, for they shall return to me with their whole heart." The passage is not suspect from any textual-critical perspective; its uniqueness lies in its combination of two fundamental Old Testament ways of speaking about knowledge of Yahweh, ways normally clearly separated. First, it employs a form frequently found in both Hosea and Jeremiah: the accusative statement, "to know me."[48] Then, however, it peculiarly overloads the statement by adding the knowledge content[49] as the objective clause in its strict formulation, *ky 'ny yhwh*, a formulation used, so to speak, exclusively in the book of Ezekiel, This is the only time in the Old Testament that we encounter the absolute employment of the statement of recognition as it is extracted from the referential structure we described in chapter 2. We must inquire concerning the meaning of this addition of the object clause, a clause that initially seems to be nothing more than a tautology of the preceding, more tersely formulated accusative statement. If we are not to consider it a mere thoughtless piling on of words, then we must assume that the *ky'ny yhwh* carries a certain shade of meaning not contained in the simple accusative statement. In this extremely weighty passage (the covenant formula follows), it is precisely this shade of meaning that Jeremiah wishes to express above and beyond his usual talk about knowledge of Yahweh. In a later context we will have to consider what this particular nuance is in the formulation *wyd'w ky 'ny yhwh* that transcends the simple formulation *yd' 't yhwh* (chapter 5, section *b*). At this point in our discussion of this passage (the only one in the entire Old Testament that combines the two types of statements), the observation must suffice that the *ky 'ny yhwh* in the second position apparently contains the more sharply outlined and delineated statement that is able to add an element of amplification to the simple accusative. Not even Jeremiah uses it again in this fashion, and this is the only way we can explain its addition here.

(e) *The More Freely Formulated Examples of the Statement of Recognition in the Rest of the Old Testament*

To complete our examination, we must now consider a series of passages that formulate the statement of recognition more freely. In this context we will pay attention above all to the knowledge content. Instead of the formula, "know that I am Yahweh," we now frequently hear, "know that my name is Yahweh." This is the case in the statement concluding the secondary discourse in Jeremiah 16:19–21: "Therefore, behold, I will make them know, this once I will make them know my power [literally: hand] and my might, and they shall know that my name is Yahweh." This passage can be interpreted as an early exegesis of the strict formula. It shows most unambiguously that to hear, "I am Yahweh," is indeed a matter of recognizing Yahweh's name. In the perhaps secondarily glossed and somewhat overburdened conclusion to Psalm 83 this statement is combined with a reference to Yahweh's singularity, a reference we also saw in Deuteronomy and Deutero-Isaiah:

> Let them [the enemies] be put to shame . . .
> Let them know that thou alone,
>   whose name is Yahweh,
> art the Most High over all the earth.[50] (Ps. 83:17–18, RSV)

In an imperative formulation, Psalm 4:3 calls for recognition of the God who performs wonders: "Know that Yahweh does wonders 'in his mercy with me.' " Psalm 135:5 speaks in the form of a subsequent, affirming confession of Yahweh's majesty: "For I know that Yahweh is great." More frequently, however, we encounter this zeal for the recognition of Yahweh's power and dominion as a conclusion to the suppliant's request. Psalm 59:13:

> . . . consume them in wrath,
>   consume them till they are no more.
> that men may know that Yahweh [c. t.] rules over Jacob
>   to the ends of the earth. (RSV)

Psalm 109:8 f.:

> Help me, O Yahweh, my God!
>   Save me according to thy steadfast love!
> So that they know that this is thy hand;
>   that thou, Yahweh hast done it!

(Cf. also Ps. 67:2.) The structuring of the prayer with the statement of recognition at the end, still nicely visible in Hezekiah's prayer (2 Kings 19:19 par.), has for the most part been obscured in these more broadly formulated psalmic prayers.

Joshua 3 f. shows in exemplary fashion that Old Testament talk
about Yahweh's power is never understood in the sense of an
isolated statement about Yahweh's being, but rather always with an
eye to Yahweh's historical manifestations. In 4:24 the simple
statement of power lies behind the recognition formula in Joshua's
concluding speech:

> Then you shall let your children know, "Israel passed over this
> Jordan on dry ground" . . . so that [lm'n] all the peoples of the earth
> may know that the hand of Yahweh is mighty; that you may fear
> Yahweh, your God, for ever.   (Josh. 4:22–24, RSV)

In the discourse in which Joshua announces the event, on the other
hand, all emphasis is on the manifestation of Yahweh's nearness to
his people; in 3:10 we read:

> Hereby you shall know [bz't td'wn] that the living God is among
> you, and that he will without fail drive out from before you the
> Canaanites. . . . Behold, the ark of the covenant of the Lord of all
> the earth is to pass before you into the Jordan. (RSV)

The miracle announced in these words becomes a sign confirming
the nearness of the living God.

However, the particular locale at which Yahweh encounters his
people again and again is his Word. In the delivery of the word
proclaimed by his emissary Yahweh manifests himself as the one he
actually is. This is brought to expression in a sharply alternative
fashion by the Yahweh discourse against the disobedient Jews of
Egypt in Jeremiah 44:27 ff.:

> Behold, I am watching over them for evil and not for good; all the
> men of Judah who are in the land of Egypt shall be consumed by the
> sword and by famine . . . and all the remnant of Judah . . . shall
> know whose word will stand [wyd'w . . . dbr my yqwm], mine or
> theirs. This shall be the sign to you, says Yahweh, that I will punish
> you in this place, in order that you may know that my words will
> surely stand against you [lm'n td'w ky qwm yqwmw dbry] for
> evil. . . . Behold, I will give Pharaoh Hophra king of Egypt into the
> hand of his enemies. (RSV)

These actions against Pharaoh, announced by the prophet, will be a
sign showing that Yahweh remains Yahweh, faithful to his word.

2 Kings 10:10 deals with a completely different situation that is nonetheless closely related in its fundamental evaluation of things. The revolutionary Jehu, having seen the heads of the murdered Samarian royal family sent to him by Ahab, feigns astonishment and cries out: "Know then that there shall fall to the earth nothing of the word of Yahweh, which Yahweh spoke concerning the house of Ahab [*d'w 'pw' ky l' ypl mdbr yhwh*]; for Yahweh has done what he said by his servant Elijah" (RSV). By interpreting the events as divine judgment, Jehu challenges the people to recognize in these events Yahweh's faithfulness to his word. We encounter the same idea in Joshua's Deuteronomistic farewell speech:

> And now I am about to go the way of all the earth, and you know in your hearts and soul, all of you, that not one thing has failed of all the good things which Yahweh your God promised concerning you [*wyd'tm bkl lbkm wbkl npškm ky l' npl dbr 'ḥd*]; all have come to pass for you, not one of them has failed. (Josh. 23:14, RSV)

The formulation, "in your hearts and souls," warns anew against exaggerating the intellectual character of the knowledge intended by the statement of recognition. Recognition involves the entire person.

Several more freely formulated statements of recognition powerfully draw out one final line already seen in an earlier context. At the conclusion of the story of Elisha's healing the leprous Syrian field commander Naaman, we hear the following open confession from Naaman: "Behold, I know that there is no God in all the earth except [only] in Israel" (2 Kings 5:15). The story's introduction relates how the royal court in Israel was totally perplexed as to how they might accommodate Naaman's wish to be healed; Elisha then says: "Let him come to me, that he may know that there is a prophet in Israel" (5:8). The strikingly different descriptions of the knowledge content—illuminates again the way in which Yahweh is near to his people. Yahweh gives himself over to human knowledge in the prophet Elisha's announcement and authoritative acts. Recognizing him as the God of Israel means in this instance also recognizing that there is a prophet in Israel.

These two statements also appear tightly juxtaposed in Elijah's

prayer in the great scene of divine judgment on Carmel. Elijah
prays:

> O Yahweh, God of Abraham, Isaac, and Israel, let it be known this
> day *[hywm yiwwāḍa']* that thou art God in Israel, and that I am thy
> servant, and that I have done all these things at thy word. Answer
> me, O Yahweh, answer me, that this people may know *[w^eyêḍ'û
> h'm hzh]* that thou, O Yahweh, art God, and that thou hast turned
> their hearts back.   (1 Kings 18:36 f., RSV)

Again we encounter a scene involving the most significant of
decisions, a scene in which Yahweh is to reveal himself against Baal
by means of a sign from heaven by which Israel is to recognize him.
In the prayer, Elijah's interests are totally submerged in Yahweh's
interests. Recognition of Yahweh will simultaneously be recognition of Elijah, Yahweh's emissary.

Finally, from this perspective we can illustrate anew a
peculiar situation in the book of the prophet Zechariah that has
already repeatedly drawn attention to itself.[51] Four times in this
book, and always in the context of individual insertions and
additions to the cycle of visions, we hear the remark: "Then you
will know that Yahweh of hosts has sent me" (2:9, 11; 4:9; 6:15).
What is formally unusual here is that in 2:9, 11, these words pass
without any transition at all from Yahweh's first-person speech
into a first-person statement of recognition in the mouth of the
prophet. Again and again this fact has led to a suspicion that these
statements are secondary additions. A structural examination
that considers all we have seen to this point, however, reveals that
these statements are quite appropriately integrated into the
preceding text. All four passages are primarily concerned with an
announcement of Yahweh's acts.[52] The events caused by Yahweh
are to bring about recognition (i.e., acknowledgment) of the
prophet as Yahweh's emissary. True, the juxtaposition of
recognition of God and recognition of the prophet, so clearly
expressed in 1 Kings 18, has given way here to the simple
recognition of the prophet's commission. Nonetheless, there can
be no doubt that in a fundamental sense recognition of the
prophet involves recognition of Yahweh and his action as well.

The prophet thus describes himself quite appropriately only in terms of his commission.[53]

4. The Recognition Event

In the preceding investigation into the appearances of the statement of recognition in the Old Testament, the increasingly frequent vacillation surrounding the various settings in which the statements appear has become quite noticeable. Our point of departure was the book of Ezekiel, in which the statement was part of the framework of the prophetic saying. In what followed, however, we encountered the formula in completely different contexts: in prayers, in narrative accounts, in later confessional accounts, and even in paraenetic discourses. This shows that the process implied by the statement of recognition indeed takes place in time. It is a process that appears differently depending on different angles of vision, and in view of this characteristic it probably takes place in a specific sequential order.

It has also become clear that the knowledge implied by the statement of recognition is not concerned with that part of Yahweh's being that transcends the world, though a superficial look at the strict formulation, "know that I am Yahweh," may tempt us to this conclusion. Such knowledge always takes place within the context of a very concrete history, a history embodied in concrete emissaries and coming to resolution in them. That history becomes a challenge and a claim in the proclaimer's words.

Thus it is appropriate that we pause at this point and try to discern this concrete process of recognition, at least to the extent that the texts permit. Our preceding investigation has been concerned primarily with form-critical questions, especially with the linguistic or literary phenomenon of the recognition formula: its structure, its position within a given context, and with its distribution within the Old Testament. Now, however, we must expand the inquiry to explore what it is that stands behind this formula; or more precisely, we must investigate the event it implies. We need to grasp its various characteristics and describe it in the individual stages we encounter in the Old Testament statements.

Our analysis of the formula has already given us the fundamental insight for this description. The knowledge implied by the statement of recognition can only be described in connection with the actions of Yahweh that precede the recognition, prompt it, and provide it with a basis. Nowhere does the statement of recognition speak of recognition apart from the divine acts which nourish it.[54] There is no room here for knowledge emerging darkly from interior human meditation, from an existential analysis of human beings and the world, or from speculation. The irreversible sequence, "Yahweh's acts—human recognition," is constitutive for the description of the process. This fact advises against separating the recognition itself from Yahweh's preceding acts and describing the recognition process in isolation.

Right at the beginning we can guard against a mistaken sequential ordering of the statement forms by remembering just this: that the recognition is inextricably associated with Yahweh's deeds, and that the sequence (1) Yahweh's deed (2) human recognition cannot be reversed. In our analysis we noticed the latent imperative element within the statement of recognition. Recognition of Yahweh is always something expected of someone, something demanded. "Be still, and know that I am God" (Ps. 46:10). This imperative thrust suggests that we place the paraenetic statements at the beginning of the recognition event. First, recognition of Yahweh is demanded; then it occurs. If, however, Yahweh's deed and recognition follow one upon the other in the way just described, then one cannot possibly position the paraenetic-imperative formulation first. The first condition for knowledge of Yahweh is that Yahweh act. This can never be humanly invoked; it can only be requested. The first position must thus be occupied by the prayer formulations we find in the psalms and elsewhere.

The expectation of recognition can initially be implied from a distance in the frightened cry of a helpless person who calls for God to act. This is the case in the Isaiah story. Pressed by the arrogant letter Sennacherib has given his messengers, King Hezekiah goes into the Temple, spreads it before Yahweh in prayer, and concludes: "So now, O Yahweh our God, save us, I beseech thee, from his hand, that all the kingdoms of the earth may know that thou, O Yahweh, art God alone" (2 Kings 19:19). Yahweh then sends Isaiah to Hezekiah with the authoritative message of Yahweh's decision to save Jerusalem.

In the story of the divine judgment at Carmel we again hear this helpless supplication preceding the divine deed; however, this time it is spoken by the prophet himself, who was to be acting with such full authority. After the Baal prophets have prayed unsuccessfully for fire from heaven, Elijah approaches the Yahweh altar he has erected and cries to Yahweh:

> O Yahweh, God of Abraham, Isaac, and Israel, let it be known this day that thou art God in Israel, and that I am thy servant, and that I have done all these things at thy word. Answer me, O Yahweh, answer me, that this people may know that thou, O Yahweh, art God, and that thou hast turned their hearts back.
>
> (1 Kings 18:36–37, RSV)

The authority with which Elijah fixes the divine judgment does not release him from having to raise his own hands in helpless supplication to Yahweh in the hour of decision. Thus here, too, the act that brings about recognition is Yahweh's alone; even though precisely this act also serves to legitimize Elijah as a true emissary and to evoke recognition of the servant as well as of Yahweh himself.[55]

In the Elijah story Yahweh answers immediately through his show of power. In the Hezekiah-Isaiah story, on the other hand, it is possible that he can promise through his authoritative emissary, to answer the supplication before he actually intervenes. This discloses the event's second stage, in which there is now room for the statement of recognition and of which the Old Testament offers us the most examples. We have encountered the statement of recognition above all in the context of the divine prophetic message. In 1 Kings 20 this message emerged within the framework of an extremely tense, overripe situation of war. In the book of Ezekiel the statement expands itself within the overall literary-prophetic elaboration into a statement determining the fate of the entire people in both judgment and redemption.[56] And to be sure, this is not understood any less historically and concretely.

A comparison of Deutero-Isaiah with statements from the Psalms revealed further that there must also have been some form of priestly divine message, perhaps along the line of Begrich's "priestly oracular supplication hearing." The story of Eli and Hannah in 1 Samuel 1 is the most beautiful narrative portrayal of a situation involving the priestly promise of hearing.[57] In formal correspondence to the suppliant's words (cited for the first stage), and in addition to the promise that Yahweh will hear the plea, the priest can add that Yahweh's action should bring about knowledge.[58]

The figure of Moses, on the other hand, who announced a great deal concerning divine acts and the resulting knowledge, can be described fully neither as a prophet nor as a priest. He is rather the emissary through whom Yahweh authoritatively leads and instructs his people. David's speech to Goliath shows further that under certain circumstances a simple member of the covenant people, trusting in the Lord of holy war, can speak with similar certainty about Yahweh's help and the knowledge it elicits: "This day Yahweh will deliver you into my hand, and I will strike you down . . . that all the earth may know that there is a God in Israel . . ." (1 Sam. 17:46, RSV).

In this second type of usage, then, the statement of recognition is associated with the authoritative word of the divine promise of hearing, and it may initially appear that we are dealing here with an exclusively prophetic form of speech. Careful examination reveals, however, that the prophet can stand next to the priest, next to the charismatic who leads the people, and next to the pious person who is victorious in Yahweh's battle. The recognition formula is not exclusively bound to any of these individual roles, but rather appears to precede them all.

The Elijah story in 1 Kings 18 has completely passed over the second phase, in which the statement of recognition is uttered by the divine emissary who authoritatively announces a successful hearing. Elijah's prayer is followed immediately by the divine fire from heaven. The subsequent reference to the divine deed then throws the third phase into particularly sharp relief: "And when all the people saw it, they fell on their faces; and they said, 'Yahweh, he is God; Yahweh, he is God' " (1 Kings 18:38, RSV). Not only is the occurrence of the divine deed described here, but the event of recognition as well.[59] This account is particularly valuable because, in contrast to most other passages, it fully and graphically depicts this event's effect. This example clearly shows that the event of recognition is not an inward, reflective, or spiritual occurrence, but rather manifests itself in open, public prostration before Yahweh. Recognition is not just the illumination of a new perspective; it is a process of acknowledgment that becomes concrete in confession and worship and leads directly to practical decisions. The consequences for the divine emissary are clarified by the subsequent death of the prophets of Baal at the hands of Elijah, aided by the people. Elijah, not the many prophets of Baal, is recognized as the true emissary. Elijah's request is fulfilled in both parts: "Let it be known this day that thou art God in Israel, and that I am thy servant" (1 Kings 18:36, RSV).

We must also mention the story of Naaman's leprosy in this context. After being healed, the Syrian commander returns to Elisha and confesses before him: "Behold, I know that there is no God in all the earth but in Israel; so accept now a present from your servant" (2 Kings 5:15, RSV). When Elisha refuses to accept the gift, Naaman requests two mules' burden of Israelite earth upon which to worship Yahweh alone after returning to Damascus. Here, too, the presently acquired recognition of Yahweh leads to a lasting decision for Yahweh, who has made himself known in his healing acts through his prophet.

Other passages lack this broad exposition of the consequences of the newly acquired acknowledgement. They limit themselves rather to introducing the confession of the person involved as a symbolic constituent part of the larger recognition event. We hear this confessional statement spoken by the widow of Zarephath in a renewed association of the recognition of the word of God with the recognition of the divine emissary. After her son is healed, she answers Elijah: "Now I know ['th yd'ty] that you are a man of God, and that the word of Yahweh in your mouth is truth" (1 Kings 17:24, RSV).

Whereas these three passages deal with the knowledge

acquired in an encounter with prophetic acts, several passages from
the psalms lead us once again into the sphere of answers to priestly
acts. Gunkel drew attention very early to the surprising rapidity
with which the most confident certainty of help can follow the
deepest lament in many psalms (most clearly in Ps. 6). Begrich then
formed his hypothesis concerning the Priestly oracular supplication
hearing on the basis of this insight.[60] We find the announcement of
the recognition event—stated in the perfect tense—in these
statements of "certainty of hearing" that go so far as to treat the
announcement of aid quite fully as the beginning fulfillment itself
and to speak of it in perfective form. Psalm 20:1–5 speaks of the
suppliant's requests and wishes on behalf of the king; verse 6 then
fomulates the resulting certainty of successful hearing: "Now I have
seen [ʿth ydʿty] that Yahweh has saved his anointed [perf.], that he
answers him from his holy heaven." Psalm 41:10 lets us hear the
suppliant's petition: "But do thou, O Yahweh, be gracious to me,
and raise me up" (rsv). In verse 11 we then find the certainty of
hearing: "By this I have known [bz't ydʿty] that thou art pleased with
me, in that my enemy has not triumphed over me" (rsv). Once
again it is not a matter of recognizing Yahweh's essence, but rather
of recognizing the immediately merciful, helping God. It is peculiar
to both passages that this certainty is not acquired from the open
event of rescue, but instead is prompted by Yahweh's announcement of aid, probably spoken by the priest. This announcement is
part of the event of the divine answer to petition.

This observation can provide a transition to a fourth aspect of
the recognition event. According to the Old Testament faith,
Yahweh's deeds do not occur merely in the given hour in which the
people experience them and then sink from memory or lead a
shadowy existence in a history that is directed toward the past.
Again and again the Old Testament paraenesis emphasizes the
obligation to pass on the stories of Yahweh's deeds. Yahweh
hardened Pharaoh's heart and performed his signs "that you may
tell [lm'n tspr] in the hearing of your son and your son's son how I
have made sport of the Egyptians and what signs I have done among
them; that you may know that I am Yahweh" (Exod. 10:1 f.).[61] This
refers no doubt to the proclamation and witness of the congrega-

tion. However, if Yahweh's deeds do live in this proclamation, then it is self-evident that the recounting of Yahweh's deeds will also always demonstrate the hidden tendency to awaken recognition.

Exodus 18 shows us an example of the awakening of recognition from the recounting of Yahweh's great deeds that goes back to the earliest time. After hearing of Israel's departure from Egypt, Jethro comes to Moses.

> Then Moses told [*wyspr*] his father-in-law all that Yahweh had done to Pharaoh and to the Egyptians for Israel's sake. . . . And Jethro rejoiced for all the good which Yahweh had done to Israel. . . . And Jethro said, "Blessed be Yahweh, who has delivered you out of the hand of the Egyptians and out of the hand of Pharaoh. Now I know [*'th yd'ty*] that Yahweh is greater than all gods.
>
> (Exod. 18:8–11, RSV)

Once again, the event of recognition prompted by the telling of Yahweh's deeds is fully described. Jethro rejoices and praises Yahweh. One might also ask whether the sacrifice Jethro subsequently offers in verse 12 is not also a symbolic manifestation of this newly acquired knowledge.

Should we call all this the stage of the posthistory of the recognition event? We may, but only if we immediately emphasize that this posthistory is not merely a secondary undertaking with only derivative dignity, concerned only with recollection. For Old Testament faith such recounting of Yahweh's deeds involves a full reactualization in which total—not merely secondary—recognition can be acquired once again. We find this illustrated in Deuteronomy in Moses' admonition at the end of the desert wanderings. He enumerates once again the great events of the Exodus and then asserts of them: "To you it was shown, that you might know that Yahweh is God: there is no other besides him" (4:35, RSV). Although these events lie far in the past for those addressed here, they are made contemporaneous with the generation standing at the end of the desert wanderings by means of a paraenetic "this day": "Know therefore this day, and lay it to your heart, that Yahweh is God in heaven above and on the earth beneath; there is no other. Therefore you shall keep his statutes . . . " (4:39 f., RSV, similarly 7:9; 29:5). Joshua's Deuteronomistic farewell speech points toward the imminent fulfillment of the land promise: "And you know in your hearts and souls, all of you, that not one thing has failed of all the good things which Yahweh, your God, promised concerning you" (Josh. 23:14, RSV).[62]

One additional element can be mentioned in this context. Yahweh's actions on behalf of his people live not only in the narrative proclamation of the people of God, but equally in the signs Yahweh has given his people as fixed observances, observances witnessing to his particular actions on behalf of this same people. Recognition and knowledge are revivified ever anew from the perspective of these signs and the people's encounter with them. One particular sign in which, according to the perspective of the Priestly statements, Yahweh has sealed his connection with his people is the sabbath. "You shall keep my sabbaths, for this is a sign between me and you throughout your generations, that you may know that I, Yahweh, sanctify you" (Exod. 31:13, RSV). Thus it is no accident that along with the numerous passages in which Ezekiel associates recognition of Yahweh with Yahweh's imminent historical deeds, we also find two passages connecting the statement of recognition with the sabbath requirements. Reflecting upon the time of the desert wanderings, 20:12 reports: "Moreover I gave them my sabbaths, as a sign between me and them, that they might know that I, Yahweh, sanctify them." Further, 20:20 employs the form of the commandment: "Hallow my sabbaths that they may be a sign between me and you, that you may know that I, Yahweh, am your God" (RSV). It is important that these statements are also seen within the context of Yahweh's historical acts on behalf of his people, since in this case also recognition or knowledge of God (and of the people of God) is not acquired from some timeless, nonhistorical process. This sabbath is also the sacramental sign and warranty of a particular history from whose perspective Israel can recognize both its status as the elected people and Yahweh as the God who both elects and sanctifies his people.[63]

This interaction ought also to clarify relationship between the paraenetic and imperative formulations of the statement of recognition. We have chosen not to designate the imperative formulation as the first stage of the recognition event sequence.

Since the knowledge implied by the statement of recognition always follows one of Yahweh's acts, the commandment of recognition can never be the first statement. Such a demand is only possible where Yahweh's actions have become visible, even if only in the form of authoritative proclamation of his coming acts. But wherever these acts do indeed become visible, the imperative component of the statement of recognition will also make an immediate appearance. Wherever Yahweh has acted, there recognition can be demanded. Wherever his actions have brought about signs, lack of recognition is the same as disobedience. This holds true all the way down to Paul, who considers the heathens' disobedience in the face of God's self-revelation in his works to be an unforgivable sin (Rom. 1:18 ff.). He understands these "works" (*poiémata*) in the Old Testament sense of Genesis 1 as signs of a beginning history between God and world. The heavens are "telling" (*msprym*) and the firmament "proclaims" (*mqyd*) God's handiwork and his majesty that reveals itself in such activity (Ps. 19:1).[64]

5. The Roots of the Statement of Recognition

This recognition event implied by the statement of recognition has disclosed to us a uniquely structured occurrence. On the other hand, we have not been able to find an absolutely satisfactory answer to the question concerning the original setting or *Sitz im Leben* of the recognition formula. We encountered it in prophetic speech; it seemed to be at home in priestly speech; and finally various other Old Testament passages showed how it could be used with equal facility in ways transcending these two. Will this unsatisfactory answer have to suffice? Or is there a way to find out more about the formula's original setting?

Before investigating this question further, we must once again sharply outline exactly what it is we are examining. What we have designated as the statement of recognition is composed of two elements: (1) the statement of "recognition" in the narrower sense and (2) the designation of the content of that recognition or knowledge. We found the second element to be a variable entity. Next to the statement so prominent in Ezekiel, (know) "that I am Yahweh," we encountered the Deuteronomic formulation, (know) "that Yahweh is God." There were also freer formulations (in Ezekiel as well) that varied from case to case and adapted themselves to the context. In the first element, on the other hand, the expression *yd' ky* proved to be a constant. Aside from the form of the subsequent discourse, the verb *yd'* could be added in a simple consecutive statement with *w^e* and the perfect tense (or, less frequently, *w copulativum* with the imperfect), or it could be formulated in the imperfect in an earlier position. The final, or in the imperative formulation, the imperative component of the statement of recognition could be expressed more strongly in the form of an infinitive introduced by *lm'n, b'bwr*, or by a simple *l*. However, the fixed, basic element of the statement was always *yd'* governing an objective clause introduced by *ky*.[65] Our examination will focus first on this element, the "statement of recognition in the narrower sense." Where did it originally belong?

Since our investigation takes the book of Ezekiel as its point of departure and always seeks to return to it, it will then be necessary to examine more closely the designation of the content of that recognition so characteristic of Ezekiel: "that I am Yahweh." We have called the statement of recognition that manifests this particular formulation of recognition content "the strict statement of recognition." Can we say anything further about this particular recognition content and its association with the *yd'* statement?

(a) *The Statement of Recognition in the Narrower Sense*

The previously examined statement of recognition showed characteristically that recognition of Yahweh came about vis-à-vis an occurrence caused by Yahweh. This event took place outside the subject of recognition and provided the actual material, or better yet, the basis and cause of recognition; such recognition would be unthinkable apart from this externally occurring event. Thus the element *yd'*, formulated in the *perfectum consecutivum*, imperfect, or infinitive, was frequently augmented by the characteristic *b^e* (associated with the demonstrative pronoun or an infinitive) which more specifically expressed what might be called the instrumental effect of Yahweh's acts. "By this [*bz't*] you shall know that I am Yahweh . . ." (Exod. 7:17, RSV); "And you shall know thereby that I

am Yahweh, when I bring you into the land of Israel [*bhby'y*] . . ."
(Ezek. 20:42, RSV).

What is the original setting of this peculiar turn of phrase? An
episode far removed from the sphere of religious speech may help us
find an answer.

Genesis 42 relates Joseph's conversation with his brothers,
whom he initially charges with spying. In verse 33 f. Joseph's
brothers tell their father of this occurrence. "Then the man, the lord
of the land, said to us, 'By this [*bz't 'd'*] I shall know that you are
honest men: leave one of your brothers with me, and take grain for
the famine of your households, and go your way. Bring your
youngest brother to me; then I shall know [*w'd'h*] that you are not
spies but honest men . . .' " (RSV). The truth of the brothers'
statements will be tested by a specific sign that Joseph freely chooses
from their stories. Thus in one of Joseph's direct speeches to the
brothers the verb *bḥn* is used in a perfectly parallel fashion in the
place of the verb *yd'*.

> It is as I said to you, you are spies. By this you shall be tested [*bz't
> tibbāḥᵃnû*]: by the life of Pharaoh, you shall not go from this place
> unless your youngest brother comes here. Send one of you, and let
> him bring your brother, while you remain in prison, that your words
> may be tested, whether there is truth in you [*wybhnw dbrykm h'mt
> 'tkm*]; or else, by the life of Pharaoh, surely you are spies."
> (Gen. 42:14–16, RSV)

We clearly have before us here the structure of the recognition
process previously examined; however, this time we find it within
the sphere of a completely secular occurrence between men. One
person demands from another the offering of a specific, individual
proof, a proof the first person is willing to accept as a sign of
recognition of all the second person's statements. Recognition
comes about by means of a critical testing before which the truth
(*'mt*) of the word of whoever is tested must prove itself.[66]

This kind of testing can also take place when God and human
beings stand vis à vis one another; neither is it limited to the human
attempt to recognize God's mystery by examination. The Old
Testament speaks a great deal about God's active dealings with
human beings and is not at all reticent about mentioning God's

testing of them. At the conclusion of God's testing of Abraham,[67] we hear the following formulation spoken by God, recalling 1 Kings 17:24: "For now I know ['th yd'ty] that you fear God, seeing you have not withheld your son, your only son, from me" (Gen. 22:12). God has recognized Abraham's true obedience by means of the symbolic test involving the sacrifice of his son.

We encounter the question human beings pose concerning God and his will in a given situation much more frequently than we do the question God poses concerning human beings. Any talk about God "testing" or "putting one to the test" recedes and must make way for the humble human question concerning God's will and mystery.

In 1 Samuel 6 we first recognize quite clearly the element of an almost technical examining or testing. The chapter tells of the embarrassment of the Philistine cities that are struck with serious plagues because of the presence of Yahweh's ark. Is the ark really to blame for the plagues? The Philistine priests and diviners suggest getting rid of the ark, taking quite specific precautionary measures.

> And watch; if it goes up on the way to its own land, to Beth-shemesh, then it is the one [or it is *he*, namely, Yahweh?] that has done us this great harm; but if not, then we shall know [wyd'nw] that it is not his [Yahweh's] hand that struck us, it happened to us by chance. (1 Sam. 6:9)

The statement of recognition appears here within the framework of priestly activity. The priest is the expert who in this case knows how to pose properly the question concerning the hidden element of the holy. The hidden disposition of the holy will be recognizable in the specific occurrence of the ark's departure to Beth-shemesh, which acts as a concrete sign.

This priestly-technical element recedes in another passage. Genesis 24 recounts the activity of Abraham's servant, who departs trusting in the guidance of the God of Abraham, his master. While camping before the city of Nahor and considering his next move, he presents his questions in prayer before his master's God:

> O Yahweh, God of my master Abraham, grant me success today, I pray thee, and show steadfast love to my master Abraham. Behold, I am standing by the spring of water, and the daughters of the men

of the city are coming out to draw water. Let the maiden to whom I
shall say,"Pray let down your jar that I may drink," and who shall
say, "Drink, and I will water your camels"—let her be the one
whom thou has appointed for thy servant Isaac. By this I shall know
[bh 'd'] that thou hast shown steadfast love to my master.
(Gen. 24:12–14, RSV)

Gideon, who is not quite sure of his calling, acts similarly and tries to
recognize God's will in a sign.[68] He prays:

Behold, I am laying a fleece of wool on the threshing floor; if there
is dew on the fleece alone, and it is dry on all the ground, then I shall
know [wyd'ty] that thou wilt deliver Israel by my hand, as thou hast
said.   (Judg. 6:37, RSV)

In this context we must also mention the episode from the
Philistine war in 1 Samuel 14:8–10. Although this account does not
use the term yd', it nonetheless essentially belongs here. Indeed, its
peculiar formulation casts new light on the content of the statement
of recognition. Jonathan says the following to this armor bearer,
with whom he has approached the Philistines:

Come, let us go over to the garrison of these uncircumcised; it may
be that Yahweh will work for us; for nothing can hinder Yahweh
from saving by many or by few. . . . Behold, if we now cross over to
the men, we will not be visible to them. If they say to us, "Wait until
we come to you," then we will stand still in our place, and we will
not go up to them. But if they say, "Come up to us," then we will go
up; for Yahweh has given them into our hand. And this shall be the
sign to us [wzh lnw h'wt.].

The concluding sentence could just as easily have been formulated:
"By that we will know that Yahweh has given them into our hand."[69]
The passage has chosen the objective phrase zh lnw h'wt instead of
the subjective statement of recognition. Can we now legitimately
circumscribe this and say that recognition means letting oneself be
assured of something by means of a sign?[70]

The activity in these last examples is similar to that of the
priests and diviners; the human being actively orders the individual
circumstances that will disclose the divine message and then
presents them to God. However, we also encounter the case of

helpless questioning: "How am I to know [*bmh'd'*]?" Abraham asks this in Genesis 15:8 when he is given the incredible promise of possessing land in the future. Moses asks the same question when under the burden of his great task he wishes to assure himself of his Lord's steadfast love; he then also immediately requests that God show this steadfast love by going with Israel (Exod. 33:16).[71] The unbelieving Zechariah asks a similar question in the New Testament story of promise (Luke 1:18). 2 Kings 20:8 also belongs here even though it avoids the term *yd'*. The prophet Isaiah has just predicted that Hezekiah's illness will be healed, and Hezekiah asks: "What shall be the sign that Yahweh will heal me [*mh'wt ky yrp' yhwh ly*]?" *mh'wt* here corresponds exactly to the *bmh'd'* used elsewhere. And the prophet's answer ("This is the sign to you from Yahweh, that Yahweh will do the thing that he has promised [*zh lk h'wt m't yhwh*]") corresponds to the statement normally used, "Thereby shall you know that . . . [*bz'ttd'*]."[72] In each instance a tangible proof is to guarantee human knowledge. The person wants to recognize the validity of the divine message by means of a sign.

The last passage discussed above leads us once again to the prophetic sphere. In Israel, the occurrence in which Yahweh's truth and the validity of his word symbolically prove themselves is inevitably the event announced by the man of God.[73] Recognition here is no longer left to human arbitrariness; it is commanded. After scolding and setting the people right, Samuel ends his farewell speech with the words:

> Is it not wheat harvest today? I will call upon Yahweh, that he may send thunder and rain; and you shall know and see that your wickedness is great, which you have done in the sight of Yahweh, in asking for yourselves a king. (1 Sam. 12:17, RSV)

Recognition of Yahweh is in this case the same as recognition of one's own guilt. The act of recognition must become an act of penitence. When thunder and rain then come from heaven, "all the people greatly feared Yahweh and Samuel." We cannot miss the similarity between this scene and that on Carmel involving Elijah's divine judgment and the recognition event reported there.

We are now in a position to venture some observations concerning the statement of recognition. The material we have examined strongly suggests that the statement of recognition in the narrower sense originally belonged in the context of symbolic events. If this is true, then we can effortlessly clarify an observation that initially threatened to remain an embarrassment. This explains why the recognition formula was exclusively limited neither to the prophetic nor to the priestly sphere, but rather appeared in passages transcending them as well. The formula was originally related exclusively neither to the priestly nor to the prophetic sphere as such. It does indeed, however, demonstrate an original inclination to any context in which decisions are made or ambiguous situations are clarified by means of symbolic events. To the extent that this is the case in either the priestly or prophetic sphere, the formula will be able to make itself at home. But it always retains the freedom to make itself at home in contexts other than these two in which the same kind of decisions are made, for example, in forensic situations where decisions are rendered possible by means of proofs.

A sign in the Old Testament sense is not normally able to offer differentiated individual information, but rather manifests from the very start a certain alternative character. It decides between two possibilities.[74] Have Joseph's brothers spoken truthfully or not? Is Yahweh (or his ark) the cause of the plagues in the Philistine cities or not? (If he is not, then the Philistines are just as helpless as before, and will try to figure out other means to end the plagues.) Is Gideon really called or not? Should Jonathan and his page risk an open attack on the Philistine garrison or not? Have the Israelites sinned by demanding a king or not? Thus the recognition expressed by the recognition formula within the sphere of symbolic events will always be characterized by a certain element of alternative decision.

In light of these observations it is now not at all surprising that the statement of recognition appears with particular frequency in the stories of Moses and the Exodus from Egypt. In a very fundamental sense it is determined by means of signs and wonders that Yahweh, and not Pharaoh and his Egyptian gods, is Lord. This determination is ultimately made manifest when the Egyptians are engulfed by the Reed Sea. Jethro will acknowledge this decision on the basis of Moses' story (Exod. 18:11). However, even internal decisions involving the murmuring people or the rebellious tribe of Dathan and Abiram are resolved respectively by means of the gift of quail and manna and by means of divine judgment against the rebels. In these events the people recognize who is Lord and who is this Lord's emissary.

It is only a short distance from these decisions in Israel's early history to those in its later wars. The holy war is not a secular event; rather it is the locus of divine decision, of the symbolic manifestation of God's strength and of his elected people. We thus hear of the recognition of Yahweh not only during the miraculous crossing of the Jordan, but also during David's battle with Goliath and in Hezekiah's prayer concerning Sennacherib's threat. Should we not also understand the appearance of the formula in the speech of the prophets in this context? One characteristic of holy war was that one did not move into battle on one's own determination, but rather first discerned Yahweh's will. Yahweh then announced the battle's outcome through the mouth of his prophet.[75] Just as in the accounts of Moses, the determining sign in the alternative decision is not subsequently recognized; rather it is announced in anticipation. This removes the coming sign, the expected victory, from the realm of irrational external historical occurrences and renders it meaningful in relationship to a particular recognition process. This anchoring of the statement of recognition will also be of no small consequence for our understanding of the book of Ezekiel. It gives the historical event caused by Yahweh the status of a decision-making sign directed at human recognition.

Its employment in priestly speech can also easily be understood from the perspective of these observations. Whereas the prophet spoke within the context of the great decisions affecting the people as a whole, the priest at the sanctuary seems to have been more the protector and giver of divine counsel to the individual.[76] Individuals are also involved in situations of decision in which it is determined whether they are standing in God's love or in his wrath, whether they are guilty or innocent, whether they receive life or death, whether they are accepted or excluded from the sanctuary and the celebrating congregation. However, here also the priest speaks the supplication answer with Yahweh's full authority, and the external sign (recovery from sickness; the gift of a child in 1 Samuel 1; destruction of enemies, Pss. 83:17; 59:13; 4:3) plays no insignificant role. Here, too, is a place where the statement of recognition, associated with symbolic proof events, can take hold.

Let us summarize our observations. Our investigation has shown clearly that the statement of recognition (yd') does not originally belong, as one might initially assume, in the sphere of transmission of doctrine, either priestly-d't[77] or wisdom-d't.[78] It is not concerned with the knowing and learning of the timelessly true postulates of some doctrinal edifice.

In its original sense it stands rather in the context of proof signs. It plays a special role in the interpersonal sphere of trial proceedings in which decisions are made concerning guilt and innocence, wrong and right, on the basis of whatever proofs are presented. Deutero-Isaiah's trial discourses reflect this usage by figuratively transferring it to the legal dispute between Yahweh and the other gods.

The statement of recognition quite likely acquired considerable weight very early in the religious sphere in the context of an inquiry to God. 1 Samuel 6 suggests that it was also at home in the extrabiblical presentation of signs. A person watches for a particular event to occur, perhaps without even knowing the details beforehand ("how shall I know"). In another case the person might expect it under the auspices of specific questioning and might nominally prepare for it; finally, it may also be openly announced by someone authorized to do so. In any case, the arrival of this event is the mediator and proof of a particular recognition process. Such signs occur with extreme frequency in battle situations. In Israel they can affirm or prove Yahweh's lordship or the validity of a particular person's commission. They bring about recognition that is simultaneously always acknowledgement.

From the perspective of its origin, then, the statement of recognition has a strong element of historical decision that is by no means, however, the free product of human will. It is determined again and again by an external sign; it is prompted by that sign and is possible only as its consequence. Indeed, it is impossible to understand apart from this *factum externum*.[79]

(b) *The Strict Statement of Recognition*

In many passages the formulation of the content of recognition flows effortlessly and unproblematically from the immediate narrative context. In the dispute with Baal, Elijah asks for Yahweh's intervention "that this people may know that thou, O Yahweh, art God, and that thou hast turned their hearts back" (1 Kings 18:37, RSV). In the face of the Assyrian threat, Hezekiah asks for deliverance "that all the kingdoms of the earth may know that thou, O Yahweh, art God alone" (2 Kings 19:19, RSV). Yahweh threatens Pharaoh with multiple plagues "that you may know that there is none like me in all the earth" (Exod. 9:14, RSV). All these passages make a predicate statement about the subject Yahweh. Through his intervention Yahweh shows that he is God, the only and incomparable God.

However, in addition we encountered an extremely tight manner of expression structured in a completely different way not only in the prophetic sphere (1 Kings 20; Ezek.), but in the priestly as well (priestly oracular supplication answer behind the words of Deutero-Isaiah). In the description of the recognition content, we found that Yahweh names himself subject using the first person singular pronoun; the predicate statement next says that he is Yahweh. This formula was then able to generate all sorts of variations, though they all contained the strict formulation as a backdrop.

If one unaffectedly reflects on what has just been said, one finds it actually quite remarkable. Why does the statement of recognition not simply state "and they will know me," particularly since Yahweh speaks in the first person? Why does it insist on the ponderous and awkward phrasing "know that I am Yahweh"? One cannot object that the manner of speech that makes Yahweh into the simple object of recognition is unfamiliar and uncommon. We saw in an earlier context that it was quite possible and even well-entrenched in both Hosea and Jeremiah. Why, then, does it occur so infrequently and in such limited contexts? Since the statement of recognition occurs so extraordinarily often in Ezekiel, why does he not use the opportunity to exchange and substitute the two alternative possibilities at will? After all, it was precisely in the book of Ezekiel that we saw such rich variations and expansions of the formula. Why does Ezekiel hold so tightly to the fundamental statement '*ny yhwh*; and why, even when he departs from this form, does he not use the more flexible *yd' 't yhwh*?[80] Why do 1 Kings 20, Deutero-Isaiah, and even the Moses cycle (despite the numerous different formulations we find there) never use this obvious variation between the strict statement of recognition and the form we encounter in Hosea and Jeremiah that is so incomparably more lucid?

One can understand this extraordinarily peculiar state of affairs only by recognizing that in this '*ny yhwh*, which is part of the strict statement of recognition, we are apparently encountering a statement of inherent dignity that cannot be varied and which manifests a particular inherent content. The *wyd't ky 'ny yhwh* alludes to something specific that cannot be heard in the simple *wyd't 't yhwh*.[81] We must now get to the bottom of this specific statement.

For a detailed exposition I refer the reader to my examination of the formula '*ny ('nky) yhwh* in the *Festschrift* for A. Alt (reprinted above, pp. 1-28); here it will suffice to summarize the results of that study.

I found that the statement '*ny ('nky) yhwh* has a specific original *Sitz im Leben*. It originally belonged in the context of theophanic speech and expressed Yahweh's preliminary self-introduction. It is not fundamentally a statement of objective description, but is rather Yahweh's self-statement in which he reveals himself in his most personal mystery, his name, to the person addressed.[82] The most significant passages in which this previously unknown One reveals his name are Exodus 3 E and Exodus 6 P. They show that Yahweh's revelation of his name in the Old Testament does not simply remain a self-contained mystery that has no external effect and that one might then use in mystical reflection or magical practices.[83] Rather, the announcement of the name leads directly to Yahweh's promise to act historically on Israel's behalf. If one is then to recognize Yahweh in his name, one should not try to discern hidden meanings in it;[84] the most important element is the historical activity directed toward Israel of this God (Yahweh, "your God") who reveals himself in his name. "I am Yahweh, and I will bring you out from under the burdens of the Egyptians . . . and you shall know that I am Yahweh, your God, who has brought you out from under the burdens of the Egyptians" (Exod. 6:6–7, RSV). We hear the same historical explication in the reference to the promise to the patriarchs in Exodus 3:15; after the veiled/unveiled revelation of Yahweh's name to Moses, the following proclamation commission is given:

> Say this to the people of Israel, "Yahweh, the God of your fathers, the God of Abraham, the God of Isaac, and the God of Jacob, has sent me to you": this is my name for ever, and thus I am to be remembered throughout all generations (*zkry*). (RSV)

This reference to the God of the fathers, with whom Yahweh equates himself, is not a timeless statement about his being. It is a reference to the event of the promise to the fathers that will now come to fulfillment in the liberation from Egypt; it is in the Exodus event that Yahweh will really introduce himself to his people in his name.

The self-introductory formula then acquires yet another *Sitz im Leben* in the Old Testament, one that is highly characteristic for Old Testament faith. The event of Yahweh's covenant with Israel, regularly renewed in liturgical acts, probably caused the self-introductory statement to acquire a firm foothold in apodictic legal proceedings very early. The classic example of this association is the Decalogue; its preamble tightly combines the self-introduction by means of the name (I am Yahweh), the divine concern for Israel manifested in a covenant (your God), historical explication of this merciful concern as an event (who has brought you out of the house of bondage in Egypt), and exposition of the divine claims (you shall have no other gods before me . . .). We need not concern ourselves here with the particular expansion of these elements in the Holiness Code; the Code manifests a second type of legal exposition in which the announcement of divine self-introduction can move to the conclusion and function as a statement of legitimation.[85]

Before returning to our examination of the statement of recognition itself, let us first try to determine the particular significance and inner direction of the self-introductory formula. We immediately find that we are dealing here with an extremely important statement, one that expresses an event or process that is of central significance for Israel's faith. It is the formula that stands at the inception of the fundamental revelatory encounter (Exod. 3:6) between Yahweh and Moses, who is the divine tool of Israel's liberation from Egypt. It is also the formula governing the most important legal exposition (according to the overall Pentateuchal redaction) in the context of the making of the covenant (Exod. 20).

We observe further that the formula expresses an irreversible process. The statement "I am Yahweh" is more than merely a descriptive statement that an objective spectator or observer might make from the perspective of a third party. It is a statement of a particular quality in that it fixes the irreversibility of this process of revelation that can only occur from Yahweh to human beings. It is impossible that someone could penetrate the mystery, "Yahweh," by means of reflection or some other human undertaking so that the words "he is Yahweh" might be spoken before Yahweh himself said, "I am Yahweh."[86] The expression "I am Yahweh" asserts that this truth can only be revealed through Yahweh's own free revelation; it can never be unsurped from outside. This distinguishes it in an essential fashion from every other predication of Yahweh. From his works one can recognize that Yahweh is king, that he is the holy judge, indeed, even that he is God. But the revelation that he is Yahweh can be heard from his mouth alone. The name encloses the unassailable mystery of his singularity and uniqueness just as, if we can risk this comparison *ad minus*, a name is a human being's own most personal mystery. We can discover a great deal about a person externally: education, origin, disposition. We know that person's name, however, only if at some point it is freely offered.

The statement of recognition incorporated the formula of divine self-introduction into what became the strict recognition statement. What can be said about this combination of two originally different forms of speech?

We can first ask just where this kind of combination might have taken place. Although we will not be able to find any precise answer to this question, we can surmise with some degree of certainty that it occurred in a sphere in which the event of self-introduction in 'ny yhwh was of significance and was experienced regularly. We will likely find ourselves in the vicinity of the great liturgical events; during the description of the great revelatory occurrences by someone authorized to speak under the auspices of Yahweh's "I,"[87] or in the proclamation of the divine law, this phrase "I am Yahweh" was probably the fullest, most profound statement. This is where the statement of divine self-introduction was likely fused with the recognition formula. But did it occur first in the mouth of priestly figures performing some function in this event or in the mouth of prophetic speakers? Or are we taken back to an early period in which this kind of functional separation in the later terminological sense did not yet even apply? Both the early appearance of the strict statement of recognition in the older Moses tradition[88] and its later foothold in the prophetic and priestly sphere[89] support this hypothesis.

Our second question is more important. What were the consequences for the inner content of the statement of recognition when the self-introductory formula was incorporated into that statement? Perhaps we can risk the following hypothesis. In the strict statement of recognition, as we have seen, the recognition content is not the simple, straightforward name of Yahweh that might so easily be inserted as the object (and you shall know Yahweh); rather, we encounter in its place Yahweh's self-introductory statement, a statement that can only be understood in a particular way (and you shall know that I am Yahweh). Did this combination into the strict recognition formula not ultimately result from the disinclination to have Yahweh's name function as an object? Does the statement's awkward grammatical structure not express precisely that: even within the event of recognition—in which apparently the human is the subject with its action of recognition, and Yahweh the recognized object of this human action—Yahweh himself remains clearly and irreplaceably the subject. This incorporation of Yahweh's self-introductory formula into the statement of recognition within the context of symbolic events and divine judgment expresses the fact that Yahweh alone remains the subject of all recognition events—not only of those involving human recognition of divine action, but of human recognition and knowledge itself. Precisely when human knowledge thinks it is performing its own action, it finds that Yahweh introduces himself and can never be "taken" by human recognition. We observed that the statement of recognition is always associated with an act of which Yahweh is the subject. The unique formulation of the strict statement of recognition apparently wants to emphasize this structure as clearly as possible and to show that even within the human process of recognition Yahweh remains Lord. Any and all recognition of Yahweh can only take one as far as the threshold, where it then becomes clear that Yahweh himself is speaking here: "I am Yahweh." He freely reveals himself in his personal mystery that is otherwise incomprehensible for human beings.[90]

This juxtaposition of the recognition formula and Yahweh's self-introductory statement gives to both formal elements a new characteristic orientation. The statement of recognition was originally at home in the realm of symbolic occurrences. The Philistine priests and diviners, in trying to interpret the mystery of the disaster that had befallen their land, used this formula in the context of the measures they finally undertook. Abraham's servant used it at the well before the city of Nahor; he observed the girls coming from the city in order to recognize Yahweh's will in their actions. In holy war, where battles against Israel's enemies invariably assumed the function of divine judgment, we hear the formula spoken by the participants in the decisive events. David used this turn of phrase when battling with the giant Philistine. By incorporating Yahweh's self-introductory formula into itself, the statement of recognition is noticeably intensified into the sphere of finality, the sphere of the ultimately insurpassable. No longer is something merely incidental or episodic to be recognized here, but rather *He*, Yahweh, is recognized through his self-introduction in his name. The scenes in which this formula appears are void of any inquisitive, incidental, or momentary elements. We are not concerned here with the discovery of a bit of knowledge that may be quite helpful or even necessary for the momentary situation, something that might be laid aside when the danger has passed.

Rather, something enduringly valid is being revealed here. One cannot take leave of Yahweh's self-introduction after a quarter hour as one can from any other situation. The knowledge revealed here affects one's entire life and the entire history of a people. The recognition formula thus leaves the sphere of conditional decisions under whose auspices one may initially have called upon oracle and divine judgment; it moves instead into the middle of unconditional decisions from which one can no longer escape except at the price of disobedience. Any elements of petty manticism, divination, or oracular practices that might have adhered to the statement of recognition in its early phases have now fallen away. It has attained the status of a central statement whose significance obtains in the middle of Yahweh's great historical acts on behalf of his people.

On the other hand, however, this self-introductory formula has been expanded. Its original *Sitz im Leben* was the extraordinary event of theophany. This origin may have given legitimation to certain cultic procedures during which a secular speaker addressed the people under the auspices of Yahweh's "I" as his authorized representative during, for example, an exposition of the Law. Through its fusion with the statement of recognition the formula steps out of this limited sphere of solemn congregational celebration. The employment of the formula by the priest at the sanctuary in the context of an announcement of supplication hearing still very closely approximates a liturgical usage in the narrower sense. In prophetic speech, on the other hand, it steps into the activity of battle, as 1 Kings 20 has already shown. Yahweh reveals himself not only within the confines of "sacral space" during sacrifice and congregational psalm-singing, but also outside in the manifestation of historical activity. And he does not reveal there some secondary, incidental element, but rather his innermost mystery, his name, his singularity is revealed. The concept of Yahweh's "name" receives a uniquely new, expansive interpretation from this perspective that leaves all magical name sorcery far behind.

It is imperative that we remember, however, that this revelation of the name is not acquired through the arbitrary historical interpretation of pious spectators but rather through the authorized revelatory messengers of God's word. Here, too, the revelation stands closely connected to the initial revelation of Yahweh's name in Israel and the divine claims that from the very beginning were proclaimed in the congregation under the authority of God's name.[91]

Thus Yahweh's revelation through his present historical activity is not mentioned as something secondary, incidental, or inferior to the more important occurrences in the congregation's cult and proclamation. Just as the phrase "I am Yahweh" dominated the exposition of covenantal law in the congregation, so also does it dominate both the announcement of supplication hearing to the individual and the prophetic proclamation to the people. "Behold, I give them into your hand, and you shall know that I am Yahweh."

This strongly personalizes the historical experience both of Israel as a whole and of the individual Israelites who receives the divine word from the priest. No matter how significant and irreplaceable the stories of the great initial encounters may be, Israel and the individual Israelite do not have to return to some limited, isolated initial salvation history in order to encounter Yahweh. Instead Yahweh wants to encounter them unexpectedly in the midst of their present situation by means of his personal self-introduction in the word of his authorized emissary. In the word of the proclaimer, both the present history proclaimed by the prophet as well as the event of supplication hearing in an individual's life announced by the priest become events of Yahweh's personal address.

6. Consequences for the Overall Understanding of the Prophetic Word in the Book of Ezekiel

Returning now to the book of Ezekiel, we can use these insights to make a few general observations.

Let us reconsider the statistical information we presented at the beginning. In none of the other preexilic written prophets do we encounter the statement of recognition in its strict form. We come close to it in Hosea, who says a great deal about knowledge of Yahweh and it is all the more surprising when it never actually appears. Jeremiah uses it once (24:7) as an aid in interpreting more closely the initially predominant accusative formulation. And that is all.[92] Only Deutero-Isaiah and Joel show any clear influence of the formula; the passage in Malachi remains uncertain. This clearly shows that the book of Ezekiel, despite its unmistakable association with the older written prophecy,[93] stands in its tradition history on a completely different track. We can follow the prophetic tradition from which it emerges through 1 Kings 20 back into the northern Israelite national prophetic circles.

As far as content is concerned, our second observation is much more significant. An enormous number of passages in Ezekiel are oriented toward the statement of recognition; this high frequency betrays the fact that the knowledge of Yahweh coming about in the worshiping confession, Yahweh is God (1 Kings 18), represents a fulcral concern both of Ezekiel and of the circle dependent on him that edited his book.[94] Their highest concern is neither the restoration of a healthy people nor the reestablishment of social balance within the people; rather it is above all else the adoration that kneels because of divinely inspired recognition, an orientation toward the one who himself says "I am Yahweh." The majority of the statements are concerned with the recognition that is to take place within the people Israel. Beyond that, however, we see that this same recognition is expected from the rest of the world's nations. In this Ezekiel is similar to Deutero-Isaiah.

Our investigation concerning the statement of recognition has also clearly shown that despite a plethora of statements Ezekiel makes about recognition of God, an inquiry into Ezekiel concerning the psychological processes involved in recognition of Yahweh does not seem very promising. This kind of questioning will always remain unproductive. By his very choice of the long fixed form of the strict statement of recognition, Ezekiel makes it clear that for him none of the preconditions for recognition of Yahweh reside in human beings or in any preliminary human understanding; they lie totally within the divine initiative. Human recognition and knowledge emerge vis à vis Yahweh's actions and are realized by Yahweh's own self-introduction to human beings: "I am Yahweh." This is the only manner of recognition or knowledge about which the book of Ezekiel speaks.

Another consequence is that recognition of God cannot be attained along the path of conceptual reflection, an analysis of the world's being and of its cause, an analysis of human existence, or that of an illumination of the world through myth. This knowledge emerges only from the encounter with Yahweh's self-manifestation as authoritatively proclaimed by the emissary of the divine. There Yahweh introduces himself in his own action and calls one to worship. Understood along with the statement of recognition in terms of potential recognition of Yahweh, this self-manifestation takes on the features either of divine judgment or of a symbolically instructing divine deed that carries with it an element of decision. The prophetic word announces that what happens to Israel historically[95] is in fact Yahweh's own dealing with both his people and the nations; as such it is a *factum externum* only to the extent that it simultaneously always becomes a *verbum externum*, a word coming externally in which Yahweh speaks to Israel. This proclaimed event is the only basis for recognition of Yahweh. Yahweh introduces himself in his name as this externally intervening One, and he can be described in his personal mystery only from the perspective of this externally approaching event.

On the other hand, however, the tenacious accumulation of statements of recognition makes it perfectly clear that the events Yahweh causes to befall Israel—no matter how objectively and graphically they may be reported as external, world-historical events—are by no means to be understood as mere external history. This external event the prophet proclaims has an intended, purposeful character, and it fully realizes that character only when it elicits an event of human recognition. The prophet predicts these events with such seeming unaffected objectivity that one might mistake him for a soothsayer or clairvoyant who anticipates the future. However, these events are directed toward the people of God and are meant to elicit both recognition and worship. "Now I know that Yahweh is God" will have to be the answer of whoever hears of or then experiences these events. In this kind of answer that person will be confronted with him who personally reveals himself in his name, with the Lord both of Israel and of the individual in Israel. The person will never, however, be able to turn away with this knowledge into an ahistorical awareness or into a spiritual sphere that transcends the historical. Rather, precisely this recognition of Yahweh vis à vis the historical encounter will hold the person fast.

In Ezekiel the statement of recognition's concreteness within history is demonstrated in yet another context. Our examination of the statement of recognition's prehistory not only in the Elijah and Elisha stories, but also in the account of Moses' struggle against Dathan and Abiram, showed us that the recognition content also includes the recognition of Yahweh's emissary. Yahweh does not act in some hidden transcendence, but rather invariably through the authorized emissaries who carry his word to the people. This same element is at work in Ezekiel; in the account of his call we read: "You shall say to them, 'Thus says Yahweh.' And whether they hear or refuse to hear (for they are a rebellious house) they will know that there has been a prophet among them" (2:4 f., RSV). The same thing happens when Ezekiel apparently complains that the people do indeed listen to his words as a kind of idle pastime but that they do not act according to them. Yahweh answers: "When this comes [bb'h]—and come it will!—then they will know that a prophet has been among them" (33:33, RSV). Since Yahweh's actions are never isolated from the proclaiming word of the prophet, recognition and acknowledgment of Yahweh will always include recognition and acknowledgment of the prophet, the person so inseparable from the word event itself.

In the book of Ezekiel just as in all Old Testament prophecy, the divine event that is intended to elicit recognition is an act of Yahweh announced by the prophetic word.[96] Hence the statement of recognition can be expanded: "You shall know that I, Yahweh, have spoken" (17:21, RSV). However, this word can neither be separated from the event to which it alludes, nor, even worse, be played off against the event.[97] The expansion of the formula makes this clear: "You shall know that I, Yahweh, have spoken, and I have done it" (37:14, RSV): or "They shall know that I, Yahweh, have not spoken in vain" (6:10, RSV).[98] We must also include here those concluding short formulations that unquestionably express the same content, though employing the term yd': "I, Yahweh, have spoken, and I will do it" (17:24; 22:14; 36:36). The divine action is an event that pushes from word to reality, an occurrence pulled from anonymity by its accompanying proclamation; as such, it moves through the messenger into an encounter with the people and demands from them acknowledgment of the God manifesting himself in this proclaimed event.

Let us summarize our findings for the book of Ezekiel. By virtue of its use of the strict statement of recognition, we conclude that the book stands in an older prophetic tradition; however, its much more frequent use of the statement of recognition not only exhibits, but also draws heavily from the statement's many possibilities for variation. The limitations of the original symbolic inquiry have completely receded. The strict formulation of the recognition formula has become a tool with which one can assimilate the comprehensive process of recognition of Yahweh that is so significant for Israel's faith. It gives the prophetic word the opportunity to show emphatically that any divine activity the prophet proclaims involves the whole person, calling forth both recognition and obedience; never is it merely a piece of history that unfolds before God for its own sake. Within that history both the entire people of Israel and the individual Israelite are not merely one factor among others, but are rather a personally addressed "thou." Should we speak here about the "*pro me*" manifested in all announcements of divine activity?[99] The prophetic word, as much as it invariably appears to speak about coming historical occurrences, knows nothing of a mere objectively unfolding history; rather it is always concerned with history in which Yahweh addresses human beings. This structure of prophetic historical announcement is expressed with particular clarity by the prophetic saying that either begins or ends with the statement of recognition.

7. The Content of the Recognition of Yahweh According to the Book of Ezekiel

The previous discussion has not even touched on the final, most important question: Who is this Yahweh? What kind of Lord is introduced in his personal mystery by means of the activity announced by the prophetic book of Ezekiel?[100]

We will now attempt to outline briefly the content of Yahweh's self-introduction on the basis of the words contained in the statement of recognition;[101] our point of departure will be a passage from the older prophetic tradition in whose lineage Ezekiel unmistakably stands. During the Syrian war the prophet had said to Israel's king: "Because the Syrians have said, 'Yahweh is a god of the hills but he is not a god of the valleys,' therefore I will give all this great multitude into your hand, and you shall know that I am Yahweh" (1 Kings 20:28). According to this passage, Yahweh reveals himself as the Lord who gives victory to his people over the enemies who despise Israel's God, as well as Israel, and believe he has no powers.

A passage in Ezekiel that is concerned with foreign nations apparently directly continues this ancient prophetic-nationalistic statement in both form and content.

> Because you (Amon) said, "Aha!" over my sanctuary when it was profaned, and over the land of Israel when it was made desolate, and over the house of Judah when it went into exile; therefore I am handing you over to the people of the East for a possession, and they shall set their encampments among you . . . then you will know that I am Yahweh.
> (25:3 ff., RSV; cf. also the subsequent sayings against the nations)

Here, too, the people that despise Israel and its sanctuary are given over to their enemies. At most one might consider as an expansion the fact that the enemies, in contrast to 1 Kings 20, are not given over to Israel, but rather to the Arabian tribes in the east. In both passages Yahweh still apparently reveals himself in his actions as the Lord who intervenes on behalf of his people and historically proves his loyalty to Israel.

However, this picture is severely disturbed and unexpectedly illuminated by the plethora of judgment statements against Israel (Judah) in the first half of this book. Even the prophetic stories from the time of Elijah and Elisha spoke about the judgment of transgressors among the people and even of the sinful king. The intensification in Ezekiel is so terrifying because, on the one hand, it has been expanded to include the entire people and its entire political existence; on the other, the recurring direct association of this judgment of Israel with the strict statement of recognition virtually identifies it as the locus at which Yahweh reveals himself in his most personal essence. Yahweh's revelatory self-introduction is to be recognized in his judgment over Israel.

We already hear this identification in the expanding additions to the strict statement of recognition. "And they shall know that I, Yahweh, have spoken in my jealousy, when (by the fact that) I spend my fury upon them" (5:13, RSV). "Then you will know that I am Yahweh, who smite" (7:9, RSV). "And all flesh shall know that I, Yahweh, have drawn my sword out of its sheath; it shall not be sheathed again" (21:5, RSV). "And you shall know that I, Yahweh, have poured out my wrath upon you" (22:22, RSV).

The descriptions of Yahweh's acts that either precede or follow the recognition formula speak more convincingly yet. We saw that these descriptions do not merely accompany the statement of recognition; it is rather their very point of orientation.

> He that is far off shall die of pestilence; and he that is near shall fall by the sword; and he that is left and is preserved shall die of famine. Thus I will spend my fury upon them. And you shall know that I am Yahweh, when their slain lie among their idols.   (6:12 f., RSV)

> And I will stretch out my hand against them, and make the land desolate and waste, throughout all their habitations, from the wilderness to Riblah. Then they will know that I am Yahweh.
> (6:14, RSV)

> And they shall know that I am Yahweh, when [by the fact that] I disperse them among the nations and scatter them through the countries. But I will let a few of them escape from the sword, from famine and pestilence, that they may confess all their abominations among the nations where they go, and may know that I am Yahweh.
> (12:15 f., RSV)

In chapter 15, verse 7 depicts the merciless, continuing fury of God's wrath on the people, who had already gone through ravaging fire in 598: "Though they escape from the fire, the fire shall yet consume them; and you will know that I am Yahweh, when I set my face against them" (RSV).

This prophetic word of God encompasses within itself all that so disastrously led to the total collapse both of the state's civil independence and of the remnant of Israel's worship in Jerusalem in 587. Even further, Israel's collapse is not just described as some merely historical occurrence, or as an occurrence that might stand like a puzzle over against Yahweh's actual will. This catastrophe, in which a disloyal people meets its end (particularly chapter 7), is *the* locus at which Yahweh unveils the mystery of his person. "When (by the fact that) this comes, then you will know that I am Yahweh" (24:24, RSV).

The prophetic word during the Syrian period revealed Yahweh as the Lord whose fury comes in judgment to his enemies, and who thus intervenes in his own cause—a cause in which Israel appeared secure. The prophetic word in the book of Ezekiel, however, discloses in a much more terrifying fashion that Yahweh's judging wrath does indeed fall upon his enemies, eliminating any possibility of escape and even breaking the security of his people Israel. That is the mystery of his person: this wrath that vents itself in fury for his rights not only against all the nations, but also—and most severely—against his own house. That is Yahweh's personal mystery; it is a revelation that in the most unbearable fashion radicalizes what was revealed in those older prophetic words.

In surprisingly close proximity to these statements, however—above all in chapters 34—39, though also in various concluding passages in earlier chapters (11; 16; 17; 20; 28)—we find yet a whole series of completely different statements.[102] Despite their novel appearance, they nonetheless stand closely connected to the initially outlined series of statements. Ezekiel 20:33 ff. presents a conscious parallel to the portrayal of the period of desert wanderings about which the chapter's first half speaks. It speaks now about a new Exodus out of the exilic dispersion into the "wilderness of the peoples" and about a face-to-face judgment of the godless that will take place there. "They shall not enter the land of Israel, and you will know that I am Yahweh" (20:38, RSV). Does this refer to a converted remnant? Nowhere else do we find this idea fully expounded. In 37:1 ff. imagery is used which speaks much more sharply about a dying of the entire nation. It can be brought back to life only by the creative act of resurrection.

> And you shall know that I am Yahweh, when (by the fact that) I open your graves, and raise you from your graves, O my people. And I will put my Spirit within you, and you shall live, and I will place you in your own land; then you shall know that I, Yahweh, have spoken, and I have done it.　　　　　(37:13 f., RSV)

In 36:10 f. the new life on Israel's mountains is described:

> I will multiply men upon you, the whole house of Israel, all of it; the cities shall be inhabited and the waste places rebuilt; and I will multiply upon you man and beast; and they shall increase and be fruitful; and I will cause you to be inhabited as in your former times, and will do more good to you than ever before. Then you will know that I am Yahweh. (RSV)

Then in 36:23:

> And I will vindicate the holiness of my great name, which has been profaned among the nations, and which you have profaned among them; and the nations will know that I am Yahweh, when through you I vindicate my holiness before their eyes. (RSV)

Our short sketch here must forego any further detailed exposition. A consideration of the fundamental direction of the various statements must suffice as our concluding summary of what Ezekiel has disclosed concerning the content of the recognition of Yahweh. Once again, the reference here is not to Yahweh's metaphysical nature; rather, a historically oriented statement refers to one of Yahweh's deeds that is performed for Israel's salvation and rebuilding. "And you shall know that I am Yahweh, when I deal with you for my name's sake, not according to your evil ways, nor according to your corrupt doings, O house of Israel" (20:44, RSV). This clearly and expressly rejects any motivation of Yahweh's future action steming from a new attitude on the part of Israel. Yahweh's actions are motivated by him alone. Again we hear about his personal mystery; Yahweh acts "for his name's sake."

We instinctively feel bound here to inquire concerning the systematic balance between these two completely different types of divine action: his judgment to the bloody "end" and his reawakening to new life. Our purpose is to find a comprehensive but unified description of God. Ezekiel, however, offers us little help here. Not a single passage attempts to uncover a doctrinally determinable overall concept for this contrasting action in judgment and beneficence (for example, Yahweh's "holiness"), a concept that might reflect equally both the element of Yahweh's judgment and that of his mercy to Israel. The only phrase that combines both kinds of action and fully asserts the ultimate unity of both kinds of divine action is the strict statement of recognition in reference to Yahweh's free personal mystery manifested in both. "I am Yahweh." This prophetic book offers no unified formula for describing Yahweh's nature. Not in doctrinal speech, but rather only in sequential narrative can it express what it has to say about Yahweh. "They shall know that I am Yahweh, their God, because I sent them into exile among the nations, and then gathered them into their own land. I will leave none of them remaining among the nations any more" (39:28, RSV). The statement that speaks of Israel as a tree, a statement that seems more strongly didactic, also proceeds narratively: "And all the trees of the field shall know that I, Yahweh, bring low the high tree, and make high the low tree, dry up the green tree, and make the dry tree flourish. I, Yahweh, have spoken, and I will do it" (17:24, RSV).[103] Narrative speech form is used exclusively not only in passages that look back at Yahweh's past self-manifestation, but also in prophetic proclamation that alludes to coming divine manifestation.

Ezekiel and his book live in the period of the great collapse of the Old Testament covenant people. The total civil collapse of the remnant Israel in Judah did indeed take place. The future reestablishment and revivification of the dead nation and the total restoration of the holy sanctuary (40 ff.) proclaimed by his word remained only a hope in Ezekiel's day. To be sure, however, this salvation was already inbreaking reality in the prophetic word itself.

The small, individual phases and movements of Israel's (Judah's) history recede noticeably in Ezekiel's prophetic words before the proclamation of a great occurrence that will decide the question of life and death for the covenant people. We are no longer faced with partial struggles with the enemy of the kind found in the Syrian war in 1 Kings 20, but rather with comprehensive decisions involving Israel's total annihilation and reestablishment that affect history itself. This is an event of burning judgment upon the sinful people of God (as well as upon the neighboring peoples who committed sins with or upon Judah) and of merciful renewal that emerges only from the depths of divine freedom. Ezekiel proclaims this as the event in which Yahweh reveals himself in the personal mystery of his name. The book is almost certainly referring to the historical events of the collapse of 587 and the expected postexilic restoration.[104] The prophetic word authoritatively proclaims its own recently past and still expected history to be an encounter with the divine; it sees there events that are decisive in the fashion of a divine judgment, events in which Yahweh reveals himself in his name before all the world. And it demands acknowledgment of this God who comes in history and is near in his revelation.

The First Letter of Peter speaks about the Old Testament prophets in general, saying that "they inquired what person or time was indicated by the Spirit of Christ within them when predicting the sufferings of Christ and the subsequent glory" (1:11, RSV). The New Testament community lives from the belief that God's completed and unfolding history with the world takes place in the history of Jesus Christ, and only from the perspective of that history can God be known fully in the personal mystery of his name. It seems here the *factum externum* is not only accompanied by the proclaiming emisssary, but is itself also totally a word of proclamation. "And the Word became flesh and dwelt among us" (John 1:14). The community sees here an event that takes place completely external to human beings but that is nonetheless more than history; one truly recognizes it only by understanding it in its *pro me* orientation toward human beings. It sees here the ultimately valid divine judgment of the world, a judgment removed from anything merely episodic; it is the sign[105] in which God reveals himself in his most personal mystery (Luke 2:34). Wherever the Holy Spirit proclaims in human beings the name of Christ as the name of the Lord (1 Cor. 12:3; cf. 1 John 4:2 f.), there the recognition event in which God alone can present himself has attained its goal. Despite Paul's attempts to summarize God's actions in his talk of God's "righteousness," the New Testament community knows that in the final analysis one can speak adequately about God's revelation only in a narrative fashion: ". . . that Christ died for our sins in accordance with the scriptures, that he was buried, that he was raised on the third day in accordance with the scriptures" (1 Cor. 15:3 f., RSV). It sees in this sequence the event in which judgment—the judgment that destroys sin—and free, life-giving grace combine in God's ultimate and final act. Thus here alone will it recognize the "fulfillment"[106] of what Ezekiel says about life and death. According to their faith, the decision for or against God is made before this "servant of God" who has appeared on earth and whom they unconditionally designate as the "anointed one" and confess as the Son of God. The community calls here for a recognition of God that will always simultaneously include acknowledgment and response in the form of confession, worship, and obedience.

The Word of Divine Self-Manifestation
(Proof-Saying)
A Prophetic Genre

1957

Recent scholarship has been able to clarify somewhat the basic forms of prophetic speech: (1) the threat or promise, which Weiser[1] and Eissfeldt[2] summarize in the catchword "prediction"; (2) the invective, which can either accompany the threat as an element of legitimation or become an independent genre; (3) the warning, which Begrich[3] believes is a genre borrowed from the priestly sayings. In addition, Wolff[4] has examined the combination prediction-legitimation in all its possible variations.

However, one particular combination possibility of the prophetic saying has not yet received the attention it deserves. In the book of Ezekiel, usually at the conclusion of speech units, we quite frequently find the noticeably formal element of a goal or purpose statement that refers to a recognition event prompted by Yahweh's actions. I examined this recognition formula's origin and theological content in my study "Knowledge of God According to the Book of Ezekiel."[5] That examination needs to be continued for the purpose of viewing the combination structure designated by this recognition formula as a whole, of determining its genre as regards its *Sitz im Leben*, and thus of making these new insights accessible to genre research in the area of prophetic speech. I suggest calling this speech form the "prophetic word of self-manifestation" or, in shortened form, the "proof-saying." It seems advisable not to begin our examination of it with the book of Ezekiel; although Ezekiel does offer the most examples, it has in passages already clearly

99

loosened and even broken up the phrase's formal structure. We will begin rather with 1 Kings 20, the earliest prophetic employment of the proof-saying.

According to 1 Kings 20:13, 28, during the war with Syria a man of God twice came to the Israelite king Ahab and, in the hour of gravest danger, proclaimed a message of divine aid. In both instances it was a three-part, extremely terse prophetic word. A comparison of the two formulations shows that the middle piece, the one containing the actual prophetic announcement (prediction), sounds remarkably the same in both instances. The announcement concerning the Syrian army in verse 13 reads: *hnny ntnw bydk hywm*. Verse 28 then incorporates the *kl hhmwn hgdwl hzh* that verse 13 had mentioned in its first part into the announcement and formulates it more broadly: *wntty 't kl hhmwn hgdwl hzh bydk*. Although both passages offer a slight, formal variation to the sentence, the actual announcement concerning the enemy is in both cases: "Behold, I give it into your hand."

Von Rad has shown us[6] that the formally strict version of this sentence belongs in the context of holy war, war that is not between human beings, but rather between Yahweh and his enemies. Within this framework, Yahweh promises victory to his people. We find that the disclosure of this promise is by no means limited to the divine message the prophet receives in a vision of God. In several passages Yahweh's promise comes directly to Moses (Num. 21:34; Josh. 10:8) or Gideon (Judg. 7:9, in a night vision?) without any portrayal of the surrounding circumstances. On the other hand, however, we hear that the sober daily experiences of the spies prompted this announcement (Josh. 2:24; Judg. 18:10). In Judges 7:14 the Midianite guard's dream convinces the enemy that Yahweh has given them into Gideon's hand. Gideon, who is eavesdropping on them, can then immediately (7:15) announce this to his followers without any chance of error. Ehud is convinced of the certainty of this promise to the people by the victorious assault against Eglon (Judg. 3:28); for him the victory is an affirming sign. The story of Jonathan in 1 Samuel 14:10, 12 specifically mentions this kind of sign (*'wt*) that is virtually coerced into visibility.

Other passages speak about a direct inquiry of God. Judges 1:2 will remind one of an inquiry of Yahweh at the sanctuary at Gilgal (cf. the departure in vss. 1 f.). The Masoretic text of Judges 20:28 mentions the priest Phinehas, who served the ark of the covenant in Bethel, in connection with the inquiry. In 1 Samuel 23:4 it is quite clear how David inquires of Yahweh and from whom he receives the divine oracle. Is the speaker here the previously mentioned Priest Abiathar (22:20–23), who immediately afterwards (23:9 ff.) receives a divine oracle through the ephod (also 30:7 f.)? Or should we follow 22:5 and think rather on an oracle of the seer-prophet Gad? Both are possible. Prophetic oracles and priestly ephod-oracles are still almost indistinguishable in these David stories. The content of this kind of message is also still quite similar to that of the simple yes or no answer of the oracle through lots.[7] We invariably encounter only these two alternatives: Yahweh gives the enemy into their hand or he does not. Those involved are not expecting any specialized individual instructions. We are, doubtless, peering back here into an extremely early stage of divine answer; during holy war neither the priest nor the prophet mediated the divine oracle exclusively. The announcement, "I give them into your hand," is then a form of promise that was formally stereotyped during a period in which the two offices had not yet become clearly differentiated.

Thus the archaic stereotyped formulation of the divine oracle in 1 Kings 20 unquestionably leads us back into an early stage of prophetic speech. A stylistic loosening has already begun in 1 Kings 20 to the extent that the prophetic promise does not adhere strictly to a perfective formulation, but rather is now imperfectively or participially formulated. If we inquire concerning the *Sitz im Leben* of the proof-saying, 1 Kings 20:13, 28 lead us into a critical situation of decision for the people of Yahweh, one in which the prophet, as the authorized speaker, announces Yahweh's help to his people.

In both 1 Kings 20:13 and 28 an introductory sentence has been placed before the central element of the divine oracle, though it is formulated differently in each passage. Whereas the *y'n* sentence in verse 28 unmistakably contains an element that legitimizes the message concerning the enemy, verse 13 formulates a question. The *hr'yt* in the question finds its parallel in Yahweh's address to Elijah in 1 Kings 21:29, and at first glance it appears to function merely to make the person addressed aware of the situation into which the word of God is then immediately spoken. However, in 1 Kings 21:29 this *hr'yt* sentence is taken up by the following *y'n* sentence and connected with the subsequent divine message; this passage thus reveals that the *hr'yt* sentence also contains at least a veiled element of legitimation of the divine oracle. Chapter 20, verse 13 admittedly does not contain the specific development in a *y'n* sentence, though one could easily complete it with "because this great multitude marches self-confidently against you." Nonetheless, here also by speaking about the enemy's *hmwn*, Yahweh apparently wishes to refer to the reality that makes his intervention against the enemy comprehensible. Again it is a concept peculiar to holy war that Yahweh has the power to conquer with many or with few (1 Sam. 14:6). Wherever enemies exult over their multitude (*hmwn*), there Yahweh's special power will manifest itself. Isaiah also speaks about the divine disruption of the *hmwn* (5:13 f.; 17:12; 29:5, 7; cf. also 13:4; 16:14; 32:14). We still hear of Yahweh's advance against the enemy's *hmwn* particularly clearly in the echo of the Levitical preaching in Chronicles (2 Chron. 13:8; 14:10; 20:2, 12, 15, 24).[8]

Thus the interrogative in verse 13*a* essentially stands very close to the specific statement of legitimation in verse 28*a*. The latter expresses the self-confident opponent's godless underestimation of Yahweh's power by citing the enemy's own words: "Because the Syrians have said, 'Yahweh is a god of the hills but he is not a god of the valleys,' therefore I will . . ." (rsv). Just as in the two-part prophetic speech in 1 Kings 20:36 and 42 containing only the legitimation and announcement (prediction), it is introduced with *y'n* (a following *'šr* only in verse 36). We do not find here the term *lkn*, corresponding to *y'n*, in Isaiah and other prophets (Ezek.; see below), where it occasionally follows the customary *y'n ky* (8:6 f.; 29:13 f.; a simple *y'n* in 30:12 f.; without *lkn* in 7:5 ff.).

What is new and really characteristic for the genre we want to describe here is the addition of a third element: the goal or intention statement, *wyd't* (*wyd'tm*) *ky 'ny yhwh*. A detailed examination of this recognition formula revealed that this form originally belonged in the context of symbolic legal or prophetic proof.[9] The structure of the prophetic announcement, "I give them into your hand," alluding to historical occurrences, is significantly altered in its expansion by means of the recognition formula. This announcement could formerly be understood by itself as a simple anticipation (prediction) of coming events. However, in the expanded version this anticipation recedes into a penultimate position that is subordinated to recognition, the ultimate goal. Expressed differently, that which the prophet announces assumes the subservient function of a proof. That which is to be proved is expressed in the terse formula *ky 'ny yhwh* in which we recognize the important "formula of divine self-introduction." Thus the events announced by the prophet, in their function as a proof-sign, subordinate themselves to that which is to be proved, namely, the completely personal event of Yahweh's self-introduction. The two-part, legitimized[10] prophetic announcement becomes the three-part proof-saying whose real intention is no longer merely to announce an event, but rather to refer *through* this announcement to Yahweh's historical self-manifestation in his action, a manifestation human beings are to recognize and acknowledge. The term "proof-saying" (or "manifestation-saying") expresses this new goal orientation.

We would gladly learn more about the locus and stimulus behind the formation of this expanded form of prophetic speech. We do recognize the unmistakable formulaic nature in the description of the recognition content (*ky 'ny yhwh*), and this allows us to draw at least one conclusion with some confidence. This form arose in a situation in which the prophet knew himself to be faced with an occurrence from which the proclamation *'ny yhwh* was spoken. The proof-saying doubtlessly refers to such an act of proclamation. The prophet understood his own office as that of a servant of this proclamation's message. In his prophetic message— for example, "behold, today I give him into your hand" (1 Kings 20:13)—he announced in the name of Yahweh one of Yahweh's acts that manifested the truth of what Yahweh said at the place of this proclamation: *'ny yhwh*. The prophet's own words were thus understood as something subordinated to the primary event of divine self-proclamation.

Can we discern anything further about the locus of this proclamation in Israel? I think so. In the Decalogue, in Psalms 50 and 81, and in the Holiness Code we encounter a liturgical procedure in Israel during which the law was proclaimed from within Yahweh's self-introduction.[11] Exodus 6:2 ff.; Ezekiel 20:5 ff.; the preamble to the Decalogue; Psalm 81:10; and formulations such as Exodus 29:46; Leviticus 22:32 f.; 25:38; and Numbers 15:41 all prompt us to ask further whether there was not yet another situation—in addition to or in connection with the first—whose center was Yahweh's historical acts on Israel's behalf, the *'lhyk* that is then further developed and interpreted by the historical Credo, "who has brought you out of Egypt."[12] Elliger has shown that Leviticus 18, for example, differentiates between its usage of *'ny yhwh* and *'ny yhwh 'lhyk*, and he asks whether one ought to differentiate between the "holiness formula," *'ny yhwh*, and the "reverence formula," *ny yhwh 'lhyk*, and whether the former had its own *Sitz im Leben*.[13] He observes quite rightly that *ny yhwh 'lhyk* is a fuller expression of Yahweh's concern for Israel—than the pure formula of self-introduction. However, it is obvious that the fuller formulation, the one that expressly emphasizes the covenant reality between Yahweh and Israel in the *'lhyk*, also originates in a setting whose center is the event of self-introduction.[14]

We must seriously consider at this point whether the mention of Yahweh's "name" in Deuteronomy (and Exod. 20:24?) ought not also be understood first from the perspective of Yahweh's self-manifestation in his name rather than as a physical hypostatic introduction.[15] If this is true, then the "place which Yahweh your God will choose . . . to put his name and make his habitation there" (Deut. 12:5 and elsewhere) is not to be considered primarily as the locus of Yahweh's physical manifestation, nor is the revelation of his name such that one can now call on it as an object. It is rather the place where on divine instruction—and that no doubt also means on the basis of Yahweh's manifestation—and with full authority the *'ny yhwh* is spoken and under its auspices Yahweh's merciful acts and law are proclaimed. This turn of phrase would then refer first not to the God who can be called upon as an object, but rather to the God who as subject proclaims himself in his name.

With only few exceptions (namely, in Ezekiel), the proof-saying always employs the pure formula of self-introduction *'ny yhwh*; it is formulated with an eye to the previously discussed liturgical setting and remains inwardly oriented toward it, even if it is spoken in the middle of battle far from the cultic locale (1 Kings 20). According to the word of the prophet, the truth of the statement *'ny yhwh* proclaimed to the congregation proves itself outside the cultic setting, in the middle of historical events and under the auspices of the prophetic word of promise (prediction).

However, what in the formula of self-introduction was not originally a prophetic formula at all now becomes the constitutive element of the kind of prophetic genre we find so clearly outlined in 1 Kings 20 and Ezekiel. This provides significant new illumination for the problem of "cult prophecy." The proof-saying reveals to us a type of prophecy that is oriented toward the central liturgical event of Yahweh's self-introduction; it understands its own prophetic word to be announcing the historical proof of the truth of those liturgical claims.[16] We can only mention in passing that the priestly supplication answer also understands itself from the perspective of this event of divine revelation or announcement of name; we find this clearly demonstrated in Deutero-Isaiah.[17]

Accordingly, the prophetic proof-saying knows itself to be oriented toward the liturgical event of Yahweh's revelation in his name. On the other hand, however, it also clearly affirms the specific Old Testament understanding of this event in that it sees the proof of this revelation in the historical events it prophetically announces (predicts). We encounter name revelation in other parts of the Old Testament world; however, there it stands in a completely different referential framework. The myth of Isis and Ra[18] shows how the god's name, unwillingly revealed, is nonetheless clothed in mystery. Only an initiate can use its power. In contrast to the Old Testament wherever the name itself is to be spoken and revealed in all its majesty, we invariably encounter the idea that this proclamation is what really reveals the quantitative fullness of the name and the magnificence of its owner. Bonnet can thus assert that in ancient Egypt "one name is not enough for the gods; they must have many names."[19] We encounter the same situation in

Babylonia. The powerful invocation of Marduk's fifty names in the seventh table of the creation epic constitutes the hymnic conclusion to this festival pericope of the Babylonian New Year.

> Let them [the names] be kept [in mind] and let the leader explain them.
> Let the wise and the knowing discuss [them] together.
> Let the father recite [them] and impart to his son.
> Let the ears of shepherd and herdsman be opened.[20]

In general one can say of the gods: "[the] names make splendid their way."[21] This throws into sharp relief the economy with which the Old Testament understands everything to be contained in Yahweh's one name. Israel expects the entire proof of the magnificence of this self-revelation in the name to be found in Yahweh's *historical activity*. The events involving Israel and the world proclaimed both by Israel's Credo[22] and by the prophetic message in the form of announcement or prediction manifest the truth and majesty of the statement *'ny ywhw*. As a result Yahweh's name is neither hidden nor is its honor amplified by a quantitative and qualitative increase of its liturgical attributes. Neither does the New Testament proclamation, which recognizes the real central event in the history of Jesus Christ and thus also knows God in this name revelation, speak any differently. The God of the Bible manifests himself to the world in his historical activity.

In turn, 1 Kings 20 discloses a certain agitation within the formulation of the statement of recognition. Even though the prophet's word here is personally directed to the king, between verses 13 and 28 the recognition formula changes from singular to plural address. This shows that the prophetic announcement does not limit the circle of those to whom the manifestation is to be made to the persons directly addressed; the circle rather transcends that group. The expansion of the proof-saying in Ezekiel confirms this observation even more forcefully.

The genre of the proof-saying subsequently experiences its fullest employment in the prophetic book of Ezekiel. Since we cannot possibly follow Hölscher and assert that the prophet Ezekiel had nothing to do with any of the recognition formulas here,[23] we must consider Ezekiel to be one of the "cult prophets" who were oriented toward the liturgical event of Yahweh's self-revelation. In any case, we can discern the priest-prophet Ezekiel's proximity to the liturgical activity in the temple throughout his book.[24]

As regards the formal structure of the proof-saying we find in Ezekiel a pronounced loosening of the form and occasionally even its disintegration within the larger discursive context. In approximately a fourth of the cases we can no longer clearly discern the parameters of the self-contained proof-saying. However, even when we can delineate the individual proof-saying, the form generally flows out well beyond the terse, tripartite structure of the kind we find in 1 Kings 20.

If we consider the specifics of this expansion of the form elements from 1 Kings 20, we observe first that the introductory transitional *hr'yt* of 1 Kings 20:13 can be recognized only in Ezekiel 8 in a form that has been profoundly expanded beyond the form of the proof-saying. Four times during his walk through the Temple the prophet is asked, "Do you see?" (vs. 6 *hr'h 'th*; vss. 12, 15, 17 *hr'yt*) in the face of the abominations there. Just as in 1 Kings 20, that which is seen then becomes the legitimation for the subsequent word of judgment—a word that starts becoming reality in chapter 9 in a dramatically described scene. Thus in the juxtaposition of chapters 8 and 9 we still recognize the sequence: legitimation (invective)—announcement of judgment (prediction). However, the recognition formula which would identify the context as a proof-saying is completely absent here.

A somewhat more productive inquiry can be made concerning the legitimation speech, in the form of a *y'n*-clause, of the kind we find in 1 Kings 20:28 placed before the announcement (prediction). In Ezekiel's oracles to the nations we find a particular concentration of those forms that correspond formally to the tripartite type of proof-saying in 1 Kings 20 (25:3–5, 6–7, 8–11, 15–17; 26:2–6; 29:6b–9a; 35:5–9 [expanded in 10–13; in a unique formulation also in 14–15]; outside the oracles to the nations in 22:19–22; 13:22–23, cf. vss. 18–21). This warns us against underestimating the oracles to the nations or seeing in them something incidental to the prophetic proclamation or something taken over from an external source. The oracles to the nations (1 Kings 20:13, 28 should be designated as such oracles) are the germ cell of prophetic speech in the form of proof-saying. Formal observations in the book of Ezekiel confirm this. In Ezekiel's oracles to the nations we find the structurally purest examples of the proof-saying, a saying that subsequently goes on to service in a surprising variety of settings.

We must also ask, however, how the book of Ezekiel expands what in 1 Kings 20:13, 28 was the particularly characteristic middle part of the prophetic announcement (prediction). Here, doubtless, we encounter the most radical alterations. First, Ezekiel profoundly broadens the prophetic announcement and in the large majority of the cases eliminates the preliminary statements of legitimation such that we encounter largely a two-part saying: announcement (prediction)—recognition formula. This kind of two-part saying may, of course, have already existed before Ezekiel. A more significant observation is that Ezekiel's prophecy moves far beyond the content of oracles to the nations. The actual content of Ezekiel's prophecy before 587, just as in the other great preexilic written prophets, is unambiguously the judgment upon Yahweh's people. After 587 he announces the coming restoration of the people. It is striking how tenaciously Ezekiel directs his proclamation to the "house of Israel." Is this a specific inheritance of the kind of cultic prophecy whose setting always associated Yahweh's self-introduction with the announcement to all of Israel, "I am . . . your God, who led you out of Egypt"? Is this the kind of cultic prophecy that therefore, according to the will of the God revealing himself there, could only address the (entire people) Israel whom God led out of Egypt?

We would like to ask at this point whether Ezekiel has really preserved nothing of the characteristically structured formulation of the prophetic announcement as we find it in 1 Kings 20 within the context of holy war: "I give them into your hand." This does appear to be the case. Is it more than accidental that the verb *ntn* appears several times precisely in the oracles to foreign nations, which in any case most clearly preserve the inheritance from 1 Kings 20? To be sure, when Israel itself is judged we no longer hear: "I give them into your hand." The threat against Ammon does, however, state:

"Therefore I am handing you over to the people of the East for a possession" (25:4, RSV); ". . . and [I] will hand you over as spoil to the nations [c.t.]" (25:7, RSV); in the phrase against Moab and its country, "I will give it . . . to the people of the East as a possession [c.t.]" (25:10, RSV). Finally, may we also present the figurative use of *ntn* that in any case we encounter quite frequently in Ezekiel (cf. 25:14, 17; 35:7) as a pale straggler from the old speech tradition? On the other hand, we find a direct employment of the announcement of aid (victory over the enemy) within the announcement of disaster in the threat of 11:9 f.: "And I will . . . give you into the hands of foreigners . . . and you shall know that I am Yahweh" (RSV).

The best preserved element of the proof-saying from 1 Kings 20:13, 28 is the third, the recognition formula; this, of course, was the element that really made it possible for us to delineate the genre characterized here. Although the book of Ezekiel formulates it in its strict form in the majority of the cases, the occasional variations are not entirely without significance for our understanding of the proof-saying. Even 1 Kings 20 demonstrated a certain variability in the determination of the subject of recognition, and Ezekiel carries on with this. Indeed, it becomes even more visible when the subject of recognition is here occasionally amplified by an additional noun. This occurs above all in the passages that proclaim the global claims of this recognition of God: "all the trees of the field" (17:24); "all flesh" (21:4, the verb *r'h* is used instead of *yd'* here); "all the inhabitants of Egypt" (29:6); "the nations" (36:23, 36; 37:28; 39:7, 23); and once even "the house of Israel shall know that I am Yahweh" (39:22). A particular problem arises in those passages in which the subject of recognition is not the same as the subject about whose condition the preceding announcement speaks (6:11–13a; 7:2–4, 6–9; 12:19–20 and elsewhere). With Ezekiel we must therefore differentiate between the exiles whom he directly addresses and who live in his proximity, and the people still living in the "land of Israel" about whose condition the prophetic announcement speaks.

The simple *ky 'ny yhwh* can be expanded by an additional element in the description of the recognition content. These expansions describe more specifically the God who reveals himself in his self-introduction. It is significant that these more specific descriptions almost exclusively employ the verbal element in addition to the usual nominal statement that Yahweh is the God of Israel (your God, 20:20; their God, 28:26; 39:22, 28; or "holy in Israel," 39:7). Yahweh is the God who has spoken (5:13; 6:10; 17:21; 37:14), drawn his sword (21:10), poured out his wrath (22:22), burned (21:4), made low (17:24)—but also raised high (17:24) and rebuilt and replanted (36:36). It is he who sanctifies Israel (37:28; cf. 20:12). We find confirmed once again that the God of the Old Testament manifests himself in his *activity*.

We encounter yet another formal disruption of the original, terse statement when in individual instances the recognition formula no longer constitutes the end of the particular saying; the prophetic saying goes beyond the recognition formula—which actually discloses the ultimate purpose of the statement—into a further exposition of the prophetic announcement. Clearly, we no longer fully perceive the structure of the proof-saying in its original inner sequence. However, it can also happen that the statement issues yet a second time into a recognition formula. This gives rise to the impressive phenomenon of the double conclusion that emphatically underscores the goal of the proof-saying (30:22–26; 37:12–14).

Does this formal disruption of the proof-saying indicate that Ezekiel is speaking at a time when the liturgical situation, the original setting of the *'ny yhwh* of the divine self-introduction, no longer constituted a full experiential reality? Did the exile bring about a hiatus here? No answer to this question can be given without a thorough investigation of the self-introductory statements in the priestly supplication answer (in Deutero-Isaiah). That goes beyond the framework of the present study and must be reserved for a future investigation.

Plans for Rebuilding
After the Catastrophe of 587
1968

1

For those able to weather the storm, times of radical collapse can become times of new possibility and potential. Just such periods generated the phrase "the blessing of the nadir." The possibility of genuine new beginnings, beginnings that avoid the mistakes of earlier epochs, can only appear whenever all earlier ties have been severed. At the same time, however, it also invariably holds true that even the most profound historical changes are rarely able to break the continuity of earlier history; under the rubble of destruction elements of the old begin to stir unexpectedly and to acquire new power.

The Judean remnant of Israel, with its royal house and Temple in Jerusalem, experienced total collapse in the year 587. The Davidic royal house was toppled, and Solomon's Temple reduced to ashes. The incomparably stronger Northern Kingdom—which in a special way had claimed the name Israel for itself—had fallen to the Assyrians a short century and a half earlier, never to rise again. As a result both of the policy of the Babylonian conquerors—which differed from that of the Assyrians[1]—and of the Judeans' more extensive preparation for the catastrophe by means of the proclamation of the great written prophets, the weaker Southern Kingdom did not experience the same fate. Indeed, it even experienced a striking reawakening during the Persian period, albeit as a mutant ecclesiastical state. The prophets prepared the people to understand the mortal blow not as murky "fate," but

111

rather as a death blow from the hand of Israel's God. However, as the Yahwist narrative shows from the very beginning, Israel knew this God as the Creator God who is able to breath life into a dead body.[2] Thus the surprising new prophetic proclamation that Yahweh would revivify the "house of Israel"—a house given over to death like dried bones[3]—could find an echo among the people and generate enduring hope.

Ezekiel, already carried away to Babylon in 597, was of special significance among the proclaimers of judgment and hope for the continuation of the remnant Israel.[4] His proclamation resonates an inner tension reached by no other prophet. No other prophet declared as incisively Israel's inherent incapacity for obedience and its recalcitrancy against its God, characteristics that became visible not just after the entrance into the land of Canaan with all its temptations,[5] but rather are already visible at the beginning in Egypt.[6] On the one hand, Isaiah reflects on the city of Jerusalem and thinks of the bright past when it was still a "faithful city" full of justice and righteousness.[7] On the other hand, Ezekiel 16 insists that the Canaanite child of an Amorite father and a Hittite mother, a child not of noble lineage whom Yahweh discovered as a foundling and saved, has from the very beginning of its own actions been an unfaithful harlot.[8] From its own beginnings, the house of Israel actually can be described adequately only by the name "rebellious house."[9] Then, however, this very prophet Ezekiel proclaims the message of reawakening to new life through Yahweh's word to these people who were quite justly condemned to death. As regards both mode of experience and language, the vision of the reawakening of the dead bones in Ezekiel 37:1–14 is unmistakably Ezekielian, and it renders improbable the thesis repeatedly suggested from Hölscher[10] to Herrmann[11] that we can ascribe no salvation proclamation to the prophet Ezekiel himself. If, however, we can ascribe to the prophet's proclamation the massive promise for the future in 37:1–14, then we must also hold open the possibility that other elements of salvation promised in the book of Ezekiel come from the prophet's own hand.

One particular question will occur to anyone who considers the apodictic proclamation of Israel's deserved punishment and then the immediately following announcement of a coming revivification of the house of Israel that Yahweh will bring about "for the sake of his name"[12] by means of his power as Creator. Is there anything concrete for this decimated people to do—this people addressed by the proclamation—other than to wait diligently for this deed of new creation announced by Yahweh that only he can bring about? Israel's radical corruption reaches down into its roots in the strict sense of the word; sin has predominated in Israel since the beginning. In the face of this corruption, argumentative logic will insist that only the miracle of Israel's total recreation can bring about the possibility of a new beginning.

From his steep proclamation of judgment and coming salvation the prophet does not reach this quietistic, fatalistic conclusion, and this speaks for the genuinely living character of that proclamation. Ezekiel lives unmistakably *outside* any glass house of theological reflection; he lives rather among those of the house of Israel who sit with him in distant Babylonian exile. They patiently await the day of revivification for their dead people, yet they are simultaneously moved by the question: what should we be doing today? The harsh rebuff of 14:1–11 is spoken to those people who only wish to hear the good news of redemption; they are denied any prophetic word as long as they do not renounce their idolatrous ways. Within this word (surprisingly full of fixed formulations from sacral legal language[13]), however, there is a direct appeal to the house of Israel to change its ways (vs. 6). We also find fixed legal formulations in 18 and in 33:10–20; these passages offer concrete instructions for living an obedient life in answer to the cynicism (18:2) or the despairing, overwhelmed (33:10) attitude of those who are about to fall into resignation or fatalism or who even charge God openly with unjustness (18:25, 29; 33:17, 20). These two passages are not concerned, as has often been suggested, with developing a "doctrine of individual recompense," but rather with a direct call to turn away from previous behavior. This is shown by the way 18 ties into verses 30 f. and by the point of departure of 33:10–20 that is seen in verse 11.[14] Under the auspices of this direct call, 18:4–20 and 21 ff. destroy the fatalism of those who believe themselves to be trapped in their past because of either the fathers' or their own sin.

This is also why the prophet is designated as a "lookout" or "watch-man" who is to call the individual to conversion as well (cf. the peculiar second call account in 33:1–9; this was subsequently slightly reworked and inserted immediately following the first call account in 3:17–21). In all this the prophet becomes the admonisher who calls the members of the "dead" people, lost in the exile, to concrete new steps of obedience and directs them toward a promised future. This also, however, opens the possibility of reflective consideration on the form of that future which Yahweh promises.

2

The book of Ezekiel concludes in chapters 40—48 with a powerful vision in which the prophet is shown the new Temple of the future. He sees the entrance of Yahweh's majesty into this new sanctuary, an entrance that supercedes the horrible separation of God from Israel's sanctuary that had become visible in the vision of chapters 8—11. He sees the life-giving river that will flow out from this place down to the cursed realm of the Dead Sea, that riddle of the promised land's geography. Even that cursed realm is to be made whole again. He hears the plethora of instructions Yahweh gives concerning the Temple, its servants, and the proper distribution of the land.

Earlier scholars spoke of this concluding vision rather broadly as the prophet Ezekiel's "outline for a constitution"[15] and as such drew far-reaching literary-critical conclusions from it.[16] However, more recent scholarship, particularly the careful investigation of Gese,[17] has shown clearly that chapters 40—48 represent a structural entity that emerged from within a long and decidedly complicated growth process.

If we can no longer view the entirety of chapters 40—48 as the complete outline that emerged from Ezekiel's own proclamation, the fact remains that this textural piece has preserved the organizational plans of those who were proceeding toward a new, promised future. These plans continue what the prophet's own proclamation, as we tried to show in the previous discussion, offered in the way of concrete guidance for the obedient community that was awaiting a total fulfillment. As regards specifics it is difficult, though not totally impossible, to determine where the prophet himself was at work here. On the other hand, neither do I see any compelling reason for excluding the possibility that he still might have had a hand in the fundamental sections of chapters 40—48. We can assert with certainty, however, that certain statements in the later strata of 40—48 did not come from the prophet's own hand, since they stand at odds with statements of his own proclamation in 1—39. Even as regards these later elements within 40—48 we cannot simply assume that the older textual units were supplemented by a totally arbitrary hand. Rather, we can see a group in the priestly tradition at work, a kind of Ezekielian "school" in which the prophetic material has been transmitted and, within that transmission process, modified.

The following discussion will try to disclose some of the tendencies recognizable in the plans of chapters 40—48. Those standing before the possibility of a new beginning reflected ever more concretely on that very beginning within the course of the decades of exile. After our introductory considerations, we now would like to inquire into the specifics of just how these people used "the opportunity of point zero" in their planning. We can inquire further as to whether these regulations show us anything more of the law we mentioned at the beginning, namely, that even where someone makes conscious plans, the old tradition maintains its power and in its own turn helps determine the new outlines. Indeed, here and there it even robs those outlines of the characteristics of what is really new.

3

We must first note that what 40—48 contains in the way of new planning is imbedded in the proclamation of an impending divine deed that does not lie in the hands of human planners. It is precisely in this proclamation that we would like to see the prophet himself still at work. For example, the new sanctuary, described first in its architectural form, is not demanded imperatively as an accomplishment of postexilic temple architects. Rather it is shown in a vision to the prophet as the work that Yahweh himself has mysteriously formed, and it is measured and explicated by the

other-worldly[18] figure of "man" (*'yš*, 40:3) sent by Yahweh. It is also
Yahweh's free act which no human being can plan when according
to 43:1 ff. Yahweh's majesty returns to the new Temple, where
Yahweh now promises to dwell among his people for all time.
Human planning is also incapable of awakening the temple spring
with its mysterious capacity to grow into a river and its inherent
powers of healing. The employment of the mythical motif of the
river of paradise and its association with the genuinely Yahwistic
motifs in Isaiah 8:6 f.[19] recalls observations one can also make in
Ezekiel 1—39.[20] From this perspective it does not seem entirely
erroneous to trace these statements back to the author of the earlier
pieces.

A strongly reflective planning process apparently began in the
shadow, or more correctly in the light of these great announcements. We recognize this first in the structural description of the
temple, and the basic elements of this account concerning temple
dimensions are contained in 40:1–37, 47–49; 41:1–4. Gese has
worked this out very clearly. The tour and measuring of the temple
complex, silently carried out by the "man," reaches its unmistakable climax and preliminary conclusion with the brief interpretive
remark in the Holy of Holies (41:4), a room the prophet, unlike the
man, does not himself enter. In what follows, the same hand may
have added 41:5–15a and 42:15–20. A perusal of this basic stratum
of 40—42 discloses that only basic measurements of the building and
of the surrounding walls are given throughout.[21] This makes it clear
that the temple description is not given under the visionary
impression of towering buildings. The laudatory temple description
of the pilgrim in Psalm 48:12 f. can show how one would have to
speak in this case. The strong impression is that we are watching the
author of this account bending over a blueprint of the basic temple
structures and drawing up his description according to it.
Apparently, however, that blueprint did not encompass an overall
plan of the temple complex complete with details. We notice that
40:1–37, 47–49 and 41:1–4 give only the interior measurements of
the buildings and court complex viewed; 41:5–15a then adds the
exterior measurements of the temple edifice and of the buildings of
the two (middle) west squares, each 100 cubits on a side.[22] In

42:15–20 the overall exterior measurements are given: as regards the temple edifice itself and the overall complex, this measurement also lies behind the descriptions in 40:1–37, 47–49 and 41:1–4. The description does not, however, take into consideration the width measurements of the gate structures. What commentators have ascertained concerning this[23] belongs in the realm of speculation; it has no basis in the text itself and rests at best on extrapolations made from other structural parts mentioned in the interior measurements.

One is disinclined to separate the continuation in 43:1 ff. from the fundamental text in 40—42, even though formally it constitutes a new beginning. In any case, this section shows the context within which the blueprint standing behind that basic text in 40—42 was completed. In 43:10 f. the prophet is commissioned to say the following: "And you, son of man, describe to the house of Israel the temple and its appearance and plan, that they may be ashamed of their iniquities. And when they measure its proportions, they will be ashamed of all that they have done."[24] We cannot fail to see that in this commissioning the new structural plan for the temple complex wants to stress the radical change in thinking as regards the earlier temple structure. This is the ony way we can understand the unique sermon of penitence or shame the prophet is to deliver. The technical proclamation of the new temple complex contains no expressly paraenetic elements whatsoever. Through it, Israel—thinking now of its old temple and its structure—will recognize in shame how much it erred with the design of that old temple, a design behind which stood a particular attitude toward building and an overall concept of the integration and organization of the temple. In a way that is singular in the Old Testament, the architectural plan lying before the author of Ezekiel 42 (basic text) thus becomes the basic document of a penitential sermon.

4

Remarks in 1 Kings 6 f.[25] regarding the Solomonic temple and recent archaeological finds regarding the city gates of Megiddo, Hazor, and perhaps also Gezer show that the unmistakable "rethinking" that took place in the design of the new temple complex clearly was based on older reminiscences. This was true as regards the measurements of both the temple interior and the gates. Since I have already dealt elsewhere with these elements of the Solomonic temple and city that were introduced into the new design,[26] I will not discuss them further here. We must, however, examine just what constituted this "rethinking" that employed the "grace of point zero" in the design of the new temple blueprint.

In considering the new design in 40—42 one becomes aware first of the harmonious balance of the layout,[27] a balance that had not characterized the old temple. Certain numerical relationships quite obviously play a role here. We recognize the triad not only in the three-part temple edifice itself and the two-times-three large gate structures giving access in the south, east, and north to the exterior and interior courtyards, but also in the threefold flight of first, seven steps to the outer, then eight to the inner courtyards, and finally ten steps to the temple itself. The number seven may also be emphasized when the prophet is led through six gates to the seventh building, the temple house, that shelters the Holy of Holies in its third room. In this context one recalls distantly the Babylonian myth of Ishtar's journey into hell, according to which the goddess is led through seven gates to Ereshkigal and then out again through the seven gates;[28] however, one recalls even more strongly the Priestly creation account according to which the events lead through six days of work to the holiness of the seventh day.[29] For the rest, the emphasis on the number 25 and its multiples (50, 100, 500) is quite clear. The gate structure measures 25 by 50 cubits;[30] the temple house with its adjoining structures, 50 by 100 cubits;[31] the inner court[32] and the quadrangles of the temple and *bnyn*-aea,[33] 100 by 100 cubits; the entire temple complex, 500 by 500 cubits.[34] Considering that the number of steps (7 + 8 + 10) leading to the temple itself adds up to 25, one then asks whether the dating of the entire vision on the tenth day of the seventh month—probably the "ecclesiastical" date of the New Year[35]—of the twenty-fifth year after the deportation of Jehoiachin is not also intended to be seen within this context. Indeed, one needs to ask even further whether this date, provided externally by the event of the prophet's visionary experience, does not also yield the key to understanding the extreme emphasis on the basic number 25.

Contemporary thinkers are inclined to understand this group of numbers within the framework of the familiar decimal system. One can refer beyond the present context to the standard of measurement of the House of the Forest of Lebanon in Solomon's palace, with its measurements of 50 by 100 cubits.[36] On the other hand, proceeding on the basis of the date in 40:1 one can ask seriously whether the number of the year of jubilee (conceived from the number 7) does not lie behind this emphasis rather than that of the fiftieth year that follows upon 7 weeks figured by years. Isaiah 61:1, in a message of good tidings, speaks about a proclamation of "liberty" (drwr) to the captives and the proclaiming of a "year of Yahweh's favor." Although the central chapters of "Trito-Isaiah"[37] were probably composed in the country itself after the edict of Cyrus and after an initial return, Deutero-Isaian terminology echoes strongly enough in them[38] to convince me that in exilic circles the year of the exile's end was designated as a "liberation" and the date given in Leviticus 25:10 was used within the context of the year of jubilee. The later insertion in Ezekiel 46:16–18 also speaks about the year of liberation (šnt hdrwr) in the sense of Leviticus 25. Thus we have to ask seriously whether the date of the vision of the new temple is not intended to be understood as the midpoint of the captivity in view of the fiftieth year of liberation and whether the number 25, as the most important unit of measurement for the temple during the time of liberation, is not also illuminated from this perspective. In a special sense then, the temple described in 40—42 would carry within itself, even in its dimensions, the secret of the "temple of the great liberation."[39]

However, beyond the harmonious overall layout of the new temple complex yet another element is new and incomparably more revolutionary, and it also serves to shame the old. Again it is the context in 43:1 ff. that throws this into clear relief and offers the necessary commentary to the architectural temple design. After entering the new temple, Yahweh addresses the prophet with the following words:

> And the house of Israel shall no more defile my holy name, neither they, nor their kings, by their harlotry, and by the monuments of their kings, by setting their threshold by my threshold and their

> doorposts beside my doorposts, with only a wall between me and
> them. They have defiled my holy name by their abominations which
> they have committed, so I have consumed them in my anger. Now
> let them put away their idolatry and the monuments of their kings
> far from me.[40]

The report in 1 Kings 6 f. on Solomon's buildings shows clearly that
Solomon's temple belonged in the larger complex of the king's
palace buildings and was a constituent part of the palace design.
This corresponds to the legal reality in which the temple in
Jerusalem, just as in Bethel in the Northern Kingdom, was a royal
temple.[41] The account in 2 Kings 11 of Athalia's fall can vividly show
just how closely the palace and temple stood to one another.[42] The
royal appearance window of *Medinet habu* in Egypt, for example,
faced directly from the palace to the temple court,[43] and this kind of
natural combination of royal palace and temple[44] seemed to pose no
problems for Solomon. It apparently led to the practice of erecting
steles *pro memoria* for deceased kings within the temple complex,
which stood wall to wall with the palace complex.[45] Such an act
brought something of the world of death into the holy place along
with the stele and, beyond that, took the practice of honoring dead
kings quite unaffectedly over into the same sanctuary; this is the
kind of activity that the "rethinking" of Ezekiel 40 ff. found so
scandalous. Hence the architectural layout in 40 ff. totally separates
the temple from the palace complex, which is never expressly
mentioned in what follows in Ezekiel 40—48. An external forecourt
with the same dimensions as those on the east and north is now
planned on the sanctuary's south side, where once the palace
directly abutted the temple. Both the conclusion of 42:20 and the
instruction in 43:12 (which concludes the divine speech during the
reentry of Yahweh's majesty into the temple) programmatically
express this clear separation of the sacred from the profane, a
separation decisively placed at the foundation of the new
architectural plans.

The new temple outline underscores emphatically yet a further
element. In chapter 8, in the temple vision of the sixth year in the
period before the temple catastrophe, the entire iniquity of the old

temple organization is revealed to the prophet. On the way from the north entrance into the temple interior he sees four abominations; they culminate according to 8:16 in a view of twenty-five men standing before the temple, facing eastward, worshiping the rising sun. In doing this they turn their backs to the temple, the place of divine presence. In contrast, the entire temple layout of 40 ff.—including its later editorial additions—betrays a stern decision to direct the whole structure toward the west. The large quadrangle of the temple, 500 cubits on each side, is in its inner structure clearly *not* oriented toward the middle (as is, for example, the Heavenly Temple in imperial Peking) but rather toward the temple edifice itself on the west side, into whose Holy of Holies the divine majesty has entered. Access to the temple court is through three exterior and interior gates on the south, east, and north. The altar access lies on its east side, and the altar itself stands "in front of the temple" (40:47), not in the middle of the court.[46] Behind the temple on the west side of the temple yard, where today we find the most important entrances to the *ḥaram* from the city, stands a massive building measuring 80 by 100 cubits and designated only by the colorless term *bnyn*,[47] "structure." Not even the subsequent editorial additions say what its purpose was. Its only task is apparently to protect the rear of the temple in which Yahweh is present. One cannot approach God from the rear, and likewise one can only approach the temple complex from the east side.[48] The entire description of the temple complex is oriented toward a particular direction of prayer, a kind of *kiblah*; this forces anyone visiting the sanctuary to bow in worship to Yahweh toward the west. This is also how the editorial additions specifically prescribe it for the prince (46:2) and the "people of the land" (46:3).[49]

The instructions in 44:1 f., included after the account of the entry of Yahweh's majesty, are also motivated by the intention to plan anew in a critical fashion. They order that the outer east gate, through which Yahweh's majesty has entered, shall remain shut in the future. The custom of closed gates that are only opened during festive liturgical occasions is widely known in the history of religions, right up to the Porta Santa in Rome that even today is only opened in the year of jubilee. The material Unger[50] used to prove the existence in Babylon of a "closed door" directly from texts may not stand up under critical linguistic investigation; nonetheless, the turn of phrase *pit bābi*, "opening of the gate,"[51] used in the context of a cultic procedure, may point to occasions of closing and opening the gates in the cult of the main temple of Babylon. Similarly, Psalm 27:7–10 appears to document such an occasion for the Temple in Jerusalem. We cannot really ascertain, however, to what extent this material documents an ongoing closing of the temple gates in the Babylonian environment of the exiles in the sense, for example, of the ritual of the Porta Santa. In contrast, it is quite clear that Ezekiel 44:1 f. is not talking about a gate that is closed only intermittently, to be opened for the congregation during festive occasions. It speaks unmistakably about a gate that is closed once and for all, reflecting the singularity of the biblical revelatory event. According to the preceding account in 43:1 ff., Yahweh will dwell in "the place of [his] throne and the place of the soles of [his] feet . . . for ever" (43:7, RSV). This sharply contrasts with the ritualistic religions in which the cyclical cultic repetition of salvation history represents the real living element of liturgical life. The myth and ritual pattern, however one may evaluate its presence in the preexilic temple, is in any case decisively rejected here. A "sign" is to be sent here whose singularity will testify to the finality of Yahweh's beneficent proximity.

5

The description of the temple or its *cella* as the "place of my throne and the place of the soles of my feet" contains yet another rejection of earlier temple organization. The story of the ark in the books of Samuel suggests that in ancient Israel the ark was understood as Yahweh's throne. Psalm 132:7 and 1 Chronicles 28:2[52] show that it could also be called the stool of Yahweh's feet, that is, the "place of the soles of my feet." Thus Isaiah 6 may presuppose this when Yahweh appears to Isaiah in the hour of his calling, "sitting upon a throne, high and lifted up—apparently high in the heavens. His feet, however, rest on the ark in the temple as if on a footstool. This explains the following remark: "and his train filled the temple." Yahweh's garment flows over his feet that are resting on the ark and fills the temple. The new element in Ezekiel 43:7 is that the ark is not mentioned further. It also is absent in the later editorial expansions, for example, when 41:22 mentions "the table which is before Yahweh" (probably the shewbread table). The conscious renunciation of the divine throne and footstool of the ark here follows the elimination first of the golden image of the steer (which in the northern sanctuary of Bethel may quite correctly be understood analogously to the ark in Jerusalem as a throne [-animal] of the invisibly present God) and second of the image of the bronze serpent (which a tradition, that was by no means suppressed, traced back to Moses himself).[53] The critical new plans do not renew the throne and footstool, though their predication is transferred to the temple. This is suggested by the words in Jeremiah 3:16 f. that assert the following about the coming period of salvation: "They shall no more say, 'The ark of the covenant of Yahweh.' It shall not come to mind, or be remembered, or missed; it shall not be made again. At that time Jerusalem shall be called the throne of Yahweh, and all nations shall gather to it" (RSV).[54]

We can, to be sure, also see how this view in Ezekiel 43 is then rounded off again in the early postexilic period by even more critical voices. In Isaiah 66:1 f., a passage that might have been formulated in view of the rebuilding of the temple under Zerubbabel, we read: "Thus says Yahweh: 'Heaven is my throne and the earth is my footstool; what is the house which you would build for me, and what is the place of my rest?[55] All these things my hand has made . . . ' " (RSV). Ezekiel 40—48 is far removed from this renunciation of the belief in Yahweh's proximity in the temple, a renunciation continuing even further in the Isaian passage. Rather, all organization proceeds from the faith in the promise of Yahweh's actual presence in the midst of his people in the temple.

6

An analysis of Ezekiel 40—48 reveals that "Ezekiel's school," the circle that was reflecting intensively on the new organization in Israel after the "year of liberation," soon dealt in a special way with the figure and position of the king in the reorganized community. Any sober consideration of the community structure immediately after a possible return to the country and after the reconstruction of the temple had to encounter this question as one of the most immediate problems. The prophet's own words are already characterized by a strong interest in Jehoiachin, with whom Ezekiel himself was led into exile.

The architectural temple description had already shown that the "palace" question played an important role in these considerations. In the explicit statements about the ruler, we notice first that although the title "king" is used quite unaffectedly in recounting the misled history of the past (43:7, 9), it is consistently avoided in the discussion of the coming time and replaced by the title *nśy'*. This turning away from the name of king has its roots already in the proclamation of the prophet himself recognizable in 1—39, and it may betray the inclination to turn away from past power politics.[56] Negative perceptions that we also find in Hosea[57] and in the hostile portrayals of the rise of kingship find their adequate expression here as regards the Jerusalem environment itself.

Within this context scholars have repeatedly noticed that the prince in 40—48 displays none of the lofty characteristics of the messianic king of righteous rule that we recognize in chapter 34. This is without doubt not a result of the author of the *nśy'*-statements in 40—48 having given up those high expectations. It is, however, very likely a result of the "school of Ezekiel" having proceeded very realistically—despite any high expectations of the temple—toward the imminent reestablishment of the temple service. The figure of the prince is also integrated very concretely into the responsible planning of this imminent situation. Just as an extremely sober architectural plan of correct dimensions is woven into the description of the temple shown to the prophet by Yahweh and measured by Yahweh's heavenly emissary, so also is there a sober consideration of the role of the prince in the context of the new temple community.

We recognize even in the architectural design of the sanctuary how scrupulously they sought to avoid mixing the holy with the profane. The temple is strictly separated from the world of the cultically profane, which also includes the prince's living complex. This by no means implies, however, that the prince himself is banned from the temple. Quite the contrary, he clearly is given the position of the most distinguished member of the celebrating congregation. Ezekiel 44:3[58] designates the vestibule of the closed outer east gate as the locus of his sacrificial meal.[59] On the sabbath and at the new moon he is permitted to assist on the threshold of the inner east gate—which normally remains closed through the week—probably directly in the antecourt itself, with the sacrifice that the priest offers at the altar of the inner antecourt; here he may prostrate himself before God. The people, on the other hand, may approach only as far as the (outer) entrance to the gate building. All this clearly emphasizes the prince as the most distinguished member of the congregation.[60]

However, he clearly holds preeminence only as a member of the congregation. In 46:10 the exact entrance and exit regulations for the people are mentioned: "When they go in, the prince shall go in with them; and when they go out, he shall go out with them." This eliminates any possibility that the prince might place himself at the side of the priests and carry out priestly functions. Whatever the surrounding cultures in preexilic times may have had in the way of royal ideology and of special royal rituals in which the king might attribute to himself as the "son of god" the special priestly privilege of proximity to God,[61] none of that is imitated here. This sober organization may mirror an element of decisive reflection on the part of the circle of the "school of Ezekiel" which was concerned with the singular honor of the divine name.

Aside from the latest editorial additions in 45:1–8 and 46:16–18, Ezekiel 40—46 deals with the plans for the new sanctuary and its service. Thus it is quite natural that nothing is said about the expectations of the political authority of the Davidic line when speaking about the prince within this context, as was the case in 17:22–24;[62] 34; and 37:15 ff. One can still speak here about the prince maintaining moderation and balance and about his more specific sacrificial obligations at festivals and on the sabbath. All this lies within the context of planning toward a structuring of the new life in the new sanctuary and reflecting upon its regulations. Because we lack preexilic material that might be used as a comparison, it is difficult to determine what in these instructions is new and a departure from the old.

7

The special position of the prince is also reflected in the new plan for land distribution, a plan that in 47:13—48:29 was probably added to the older material at a later time. It logically follows 47:1–12, the promissory word concerning the temple spring that sends blessing out into the land. Next to the passage about the divine blessing for the land, a blessing mysteriously transcending all human possibilities, we encounter in this section once again a piece of soberly rational planning precisely for this land. The land given to Israel anew as a divine gift is to be distributed properly. Here we sense particularly well the inclination toward a radical reorganization of relationships from the perspective of the point-zero situation into which the catastrophic preexilic history had led.[63]

What 47:13—48:29 explicates cannot be understood merely as a corrective to the conditions inaugurated by Solomon in Jerusalem during the construction of the temple. It reaches back to regulations established during the period of the taking of the land and tries to comprehend them anew. Joshua 13—19 recounts how Joshua distributed the land to the tribes by lots after conquering the land and after Moses had already distributed land to 2½ tribes in east Jordan.[64] Ezekiel 47 f. reaches back even beyond this event at the beginning and stipulates a new distribution of land.

From this starting place let us examine two points that emerge from an overview of the land description (47:13–20) and land distribution (48:1–29). The first concerns this plan's clear avoidance of the east Jordanian area in which, according to the book of Joshua, the tribes of Reuben, Gad, and half of Manasseh lived. According to Ezekiel 48, they are resettled in the west Jordanian area in such a way that Gad must make do with a place in the far south of the claimed land. Unfortunately there are no specific explications that might help us determine the motives that led to what we might call these "politics of avoidance or renunciation." Did realistic considerations determine that the eastern areas of the earlier Israel could no longer be regained? Such realism seems to be missing entirely when the southern boundary is set at Meribath-kadesh and yet again when the northern boundary is set at the northern entrance of the *biqā*.[65] What stands behind all this is probably the old feeling, apparently also encountered in the patriarchal stories of Genesis, that the actual land of promise that Yahweh had sworn to the fathers[66] is to be found west of the Jordan. In view of the archaism that emerges from the postulation of twelve tribes—which in the sixth century was part of a dim past—the reference to an archaic tradition of a "correct" description of the land is by no means excluded.

The second observation is even more important for the present context: a thirteenth tribe, designated as *trwmh*, "offering," is added to the twelve.[67] We encounter a mixing of historical reminiscence and reformist doctrine in the peculiar situating of this tribe between seven northern and five southern tribes which accordingly would be found north and south of Jerusalem.[68] We see with utter clarity here how this land distribution was planned by the Babylonian exiles, far from the real conditions in Palestine.

But the question remains: why the delimitation and exclusion of the thirteenth land portion? Two motives can be recognized behind it. First, as was already the case in the older sections of 40—46, one wanted to prevent the holy from coming to rest in a profane realm. Thus the "consecrated offering" (*trwmh*) is singled out. This designation of the thirteenth portion by the term associated with the portion withdrawn for Yahweh,[69] a term at home in liturgical life also, expresses the humble admission that the land is in any case a gift from Yahweh. This quality of possession was to be expressed quite openly by means of a special portion reserved for Yahweh, as was customary with gifts of fields and arable land as well as with the time reserved for the sabbath. Thus the regulations from the time of Joshua are decisively altered by reserving in the middle of the country a strip 25,000 cubits wide extending from the Jordan to the Mediterranean especially designated for Yahweh.[70]

This more specific distribution of the strip of land thus singled out also refects in a particularly instructive fashion the struggle between new doctrinal consistency on the one hand, and tradition on the other, tradition that will not be repressed. The possibility of an absolute point zero in replanning shows itself here to be an illusion.

This *trwmh* doubtlessly reflects the attempt to single out from

the profane realm of tribal property something consecrated to
Yahweh in a special way. Thus it is quite natural that the center of
this "holy tribute" is the sanctuary. It is also quite natural that the
holy middle comes to rest in the priestly portion and that the Levites,
who perform service at the sanctuary, also receive their portion. To
each of these two groups there is apportioned a partial strip 10,000
cubits wide and 25,000 cubits long in what is apparently a quadrangle
25,000 cubits on a side near the center of Jerusalem, taken out of the
strip of land between the Jordan and the Mediterranean. This land
apportioned to them is expressly called *trwmt hqdš*.[71] Now, however, the tradition makes two further demands. It is impossible to
erase from memory that the city of Jerusalem belongs to the sanctuary. Thus in a kind of embarrassed solution a remaining portion[72]
5000 cubits wide and 25,000 cubits long within the quadrangle in the
trwmh strip is apportioned to the "city"[73]—a piece of land that must
be expressly designated as profane, though this basically contradicts
the intentions of the land—*trwmh*. To this is now added a second
demand that likewise cannot be subsumed under the twelve-tribe
grouping: a portion for the prince. Here in the context of the land
distribution, we again see something of the distinguished position of
the prince. Though clearly excluded from the temple servants and
placed at the side of the people by the liturgical regulations, he is also
a participant in the *trwmh*. The prince receives as a special land
portion that which remains on both sides after the structure of the
square 25,000 cubits on a side from the broad *trwmh* strip; his portion
is by no such means insignificant. Of course, his portion, though
belonging to the strip of the larger *trwmh*, is to be considered a
profane area like that of the city. Though the text contains no specific
mention of this fact, it cannot be doubted in view of the evaluation of
the "city" lying in the central square and the reservation of the
designation *trwmt hqdš* for priestly and Levitic land.

   In this participation of the prince in the *trwmh*, a value
judgment given by tradition asserts itself in clear tension to the
viewpoint of cultic sanctity. On the other hand, a comparison with
the concrete state of affairs in the preexilic period shows that the
new planning goes beyond the earlier regulations in a revolutionary
fashion and in its own turn creates a "more correct" set of

regulations concerning royal property possession, departing totally from the earlier set. In the preexilic period the royal property of the kings was composed of the property of the royal family, of the confiscated property of capital criminals, and probably also of various pieces of land made accessible by the people. From these sources there emerged land holdings spread all over the country.[74] Now there is to be permanently apportioned royal land in two related complexes, something that is missing in the book of Joshua for understandable reasons. This reflects the distinguished special position of the prince. He acquires a portion of the special deposition of the *trwmh* just as does the city, whose traditional special status is still recognizable here. This special portion, however, like that of the city, does not have the quality of the holy, even though it is part of the consecrated *trwmh*.[75]

In this context let us consider the brief regulation in 47:21–23, one that was probably added to the text at a later date. It deals with land distribution to the *gr*. In the preexilic period this term referred to a protected citizen who came from a foreign area and was dependent on the local legal protectorate. We know that during the period of Deuteronomy this *gr* was not yet cultically incorporated into the community since Deuteronomy 14:21a stipulates that the flesh of a mutilated animal cannot be eaten by members of the congregation, though it may indeed be sold to the *gr*. During the period of exile the phenomenon of the sympathetic *gr*—a foreigner who consciously joins the Yahweh community—apparently became more significant.[76] Thus planning for the conditions within the restored community in Ezekiel 47:21–23 takes a daring step into what was previously unheard of: the *gr* is also to be considered in the distribution of the land. He is to receive a full apportionment of land within the tribe in which he settles. As archaic as talk of tribes may sound here, this regulation concerning the participation of the *gr* in the possession of land is nonetheless taking a step into virgin territory. This is a daring new beginning.

8

We have not yet mentioned the large complex that breaks in as a powerful innovation in 44:4 and from there onward severs the

regulations concerning the *nśy'* and speaks about the new ones for
priests and Levites. This section belongs to the latest constituent
parts of 40—48, and it regulates the position of the priests and
delimits their office sharply in contrast to that of the Levites. It does
this against the background of a well-outlined view of recent
history, a view that at one point clearly departs from that of the
prophet Ezekiel.

We initially encounter something that corresponds totally with
the proclamation of the prophet himself in the portrayal of the
recent preexilic period as a time of serious sin. A turning away from
the old on the one hand, and a turning toward the new, pure order
on the other is, of course, the fundamental tone of the entire plan of
40—48. In 44:6 ff. a quite specific terminology for this preceding
historical phase emerged. It is the time "when Israel went astray."[77]
At most one might find a slight deviation from Ezekiel's own
statements in that he considered Israel's entire history from the
beginnings in Egypt onward (chapters 20 and 23) and Jeruslem's
history from its awakening to independent activity onward (chapter
16)[78] to have been a history of sin. The formulations of "Israel's
going astray," which might rather be understood episodically, do
not seem to express this quite as clearly.

The deviation from Ezekiel's own proclamation, however,
becomes unmistakable when in view of that preceding period of sin
a distinction is made between those who stood at that time and those
who fell. The descendants of Zadok, who were obedient to
Yahweh, are juxtaposed to the Levites, who became disloyal at that
time. In this context we cannot be concerned with pursuing the
complicated question of the "Levites" and the simultaneous
designation of the sons of Zadok as "Levitical priests."[79] Let it
suffice to say that after the investigations of Gunneweg[80] we can no
longer overgeneralize and consider the "Levites" to be the high
priests that the Deuteronomic reform brought from the high places
and concentrated in Jerusalem.[81] The discrimination against the
Levites in 44:6 ff. does, to be sure, appear to point to the cultic high
places attacked above all in Hosea, Jeremiah, and in the
Deuteronomistic historical work. Ezekiel 6 and 16 also sharply
criticize the godless activity on the mountains[82] in preexilic Israel

(and Judah). Ezekiel 22:8, however, speaks with exactly the same sharpness of the disdain for the holy things in the "city of blood," Jerusalem. The class sermon in 22:23–31 turns in verse 26 against the priests in general, and the great temple vision in 8—11 shows that the abominations had been concentrated in a special way precisely in the Jerusalem temple. Thus the judgment must begin at Yahweh's sanctuary (9:6). It is probably incorrect to identify the sons of Zadok with the "men who sigh and groan over all the abominations," on whose forehead a man clothed in linen is to put a protective mark (9:4). Those sons of Zadok were the ones really responsible for what happened in the temple. In Ezekiel 44 a historical cliché, to which scholars would like to refer with an expression used quite recently: "legend of ecclesiastical struggle," emerges unmistakably. The prerogative of the "resistance fighter" is claimed one-sidedly here by a group that we by no means encountered in this role in Ezekiel's own proclamation. Within the framework of the historical picture based on this premise, the lower service of the Levites is judged as punishment ordered by Yahweh. This low evaluation of the Levites was no doubt not the least reason the Levites were so disinclined to return after the exile.[83] In the Priestly writing's determination of Levitical service it was subsequently totally discarded.[84]

One later consequence of the low evaluation of the Levites can be seen in the strict "Levite regulation" of no property ownership[85] in the extremely late editorial addition 45:1–8; only the Zadokites are referred to here, while 44:5 speaks of a 'hzh[86] of the Levites, just as 45:6 and 46:18 speak of a 'hzh of the city and prince.

One probably ought to understand this phenomenon—comprehensible only within the later editorial expansions—as another renewed self-assertion of older conditions. The preexilic prerogative of the priests in the royal sanctuary reestablishes its claim here; however, this prerogative must articulate itself in a completely new way in view of the repression of royal influence within the sphere of the holy, something that is part of the consistent doctrinal attitude of 40—48. Here it is based on a new historico-theological viewpoint, and in what follows it associates itself with a theory of hierarchical degrees of holiness in the temple itself. Whereas the concluding remark of the architectural temple description in 42:20 still designated the entire area of the temple courts as holy,[87] and the Torah of 43:12 even designated it as most holy, these later sections place an increasing weight on the inner differentiation. They sharply differentiate between the most holy inner court realm, in which that particular sacrifice is carried out that the Zadokites offer,[88] and the outer court area, also open to the people, in which the Levites perform the service for the people (44:11). This becomes vividly apparent in the passage concerning the sacrificial kitchens in both areas (46:19–24). However, even the great priestly sacristies in 42:1–14, which served as storage for sacred objects, already announce this differentiation of sacred spheres within the temple, though the passage does not explicitly mention the separation of priests and Levites.

9

In conclusion we must mention yet one additional text in which older traditions are able to assert themselves in an extremely surprising way against the revolutionary tendencies of the new planning. The declared intention of the entire structural design of the sanctuary according to 40 ff. is to separate out the holy and to protect it against any defilement by the profane. Hence the temple was extracted from its traditional connection with the palace complex. Hence also we hear nothing more about its similarity to a city.[89] The plan for land distribution in 48:29 followed this line of thought when it separated the sphere of the city (vss. 15–20) from that of the Levites' and priests' portion (the temple court area included) and expressly declared the city area to be profane (48:15).

In 48:30–35 remarks are made concerning the city itself, which with its twelve gates represents the twelve tribes of Israel. The dimensions here follow upon the measurements in 48:16. The final sentence (vs. 35), however, contains a surprise in the new name of the city: "Yahweh is there."[90] Despite what has just been expounded; despite the insistence that the temple area houses the Holy of Holies, in which Yahweh, according to 43:1 ff., takes up residence anew; despite the insistence that the city is to be considered a profane sphere—despite all this, the city is designated here in its very name as the place where Yahweh is present. This is the old view corresponding to the actual state of affairs, according to which Jerusalem and its temple belong together and "Zion"[91] becomes the designation of the holy city. Hence Isaiah speaks of "Yahweh of hosts, who dwells on Mount Zion" (8:18) and designates the city where David slept as "hearth of God."[92] Thus toward the end of the exilic period Deutero-Isaiah speaks of Zion as the place to which one cries: "Your God reigns" (52:7). Finally, the unknown early postexilic prophet in Isaiah 60:1 ff. describes the rising of the great light over the city to which the people will return and in which their temple will be rebuilt.

The name "Yahweh is there" is now a daring attempt to fuse both city and sanctuary together again, an attempt that seems not to worry at all about what has been said in Ezekiel 40:1—48:29 and that does not really explain further just how one is to imagine this presence in the temple. In the long run, Jerusalem and its temple cannot be separated. What has been said in 40—48 is now integrated fully into the future association of Yahweh with his city, whose gates represent his people.

At the beginning we spoke about the "blessing of point zero." Despite all the new planning that we have recognized in the preceding material, planning to which this expansion and its portrayal of the symmetry of the twelve gates is added in its own turn, the intention of this last editorial expansion of the prophet's vision of the future is to maintain the old promise of Yahweh concerning his city.[93] This is not a polemic against the "rethinking," but rather it is the confession of faith in a God who in any new beginning will maintain his old promise concerning his city Jerusalem. Neither, however, does this concern take the concluding passage out of the context of the previously undertaken new planning. After all, this genuinely penitent "rethinking" and new planning only wanted—and with this we return to what we said at the outset—to be obedient and cooperative within the activity of Israel's God, who promises in his newly bequeathed beginning to renew his old loyalty.

Notes

Introduction

[1]Brevard Childs, *Introduction to the Old Testament as Scripture* (Philadelphia: Fortress, 1979), pp. 359 – 60. In *Old Testament Books for Pastor and Teacher* (Philadelphia: Westminster, 1977), p. 77, Childs writes, "It is hard to believe that this exhaustive commentary will be superseded within the next few generations." In *Introduction*, p. 360, pp. 369 – 70, Childs offers his critique of the commentary.

[2]*Ezekiel I* HERMENEIA (Philadelphia: Fortress, 1979) translated by Ronald E. Clements.

[3]E.g., *Old Testament Theology in Outline*, trans. David E. Green (Atlanta: John Knox Press, 1978), chapter 1. Indeed these essays are basic to Zimmerli's entire theological program as it is proposed in his book.

[4]More than any other in his circle, Zimmerli has helped us see the rubric of "promise-fulfillment" as a way of interpretation. See Zimmerli, "Promise and Fulfillment," *Essays on Old Testament Hermeneutics*, ed. by Claus Westermann (Richmond: John Knox Press, 1963), pp. 89 – 122. And note especially the use made of Zimmerli's work by Moltmann, *Theology of Hope* (New York: Harper and Row, 1967), pp. 101 – 116.

[5]Zimmerli's article evoked an important response by G. Chr. Macholz: "Noch Einmal: Planungen für den Wiederaufbau noch der Katastrophe von 587," VT 19(1969), pp. 322–352. Macholz follows the methodological lines of Zimmerli and pays particular attention to the land in the new "salvation time." He also follows the lead of Zimmerli in his focus on the theological intent of the tradition.

[6]On the difficulty and cruciality of the category of revelation, see Paul R. Wells, *James Barr and the Bible* (Phillipsburg, N.J.: Presbyterian and Reformed Publishing Company, 1980), p. 152ff. I cite this work not because of the arguments of Wells, but because his attempt to settle the issue on formal grounds suggests the depth of the problem. On the centrality of the question, see Hans-Joachim Kraus, *Die Biblische Theologie* (Neukirchen-Vluyn: Neukirchener Verlag, 1970), pp. 371–76.

[7]However it is clear that this is the common thread. This is indicated by the title of the collection of essays *Gottes Offenbarung; Gesammelte*

Aufsätze (ThB 19: München: Chr. Kaiser Verlag, 1963). See Zimmerli's comment in the Foreword. His basic essay which engages the subject is "'Offenbarung' im Alten Testament," EvTh 22 (1962), pp. 15–31. But the essays offered here provide the exegetical work which lie behind that statement.

[8]G. Ernest Wright, *God Who Acts* SBT 8 (London: SCM Press, 1952); Gerhard von Rad, *Old Testament Theology I*, trans. D. M. G. Stalker (New York: Harper and Row, 1962) in which von Rad developed the thesis articulated in "The Form-Critical Problem of the Hexateuch," *The Problem of the Hexateuch, and Other Essays* (New York: McGraw-Hill, 1966), pp. 1–78. That decisive statement was first published in 1938. On a recital of theological memories now much more critically understood, see Norman Gottwald, *The Tribes of Yahweh* (Maryknoll, N.Y.: Orbis Books, 1979), pp. 72–114, and especially the summary chart on pp. 102–103.

[9]See the book by that title, *Revelation as History*, ed. Wolfhart Pannenberg (New York: Macmillan Company, 1968) the German edition published in 1961. The collection contains the important piece by Rolf Rendtorff to which Zimmerli responded in his article in *Evangelische Theologie* in 1962.

[10]Brevard S. Childs, *Biblical Theology in Crisis* (Philadelphia: Westminster, 1970).

[11]The general critique has been persistent with Barr. But see especially "Revelation through History in the Old Testament and in Modern Theology," *Interpretation* 17 (1963), pp. 193–205; "The Old Testament and the New Crisis of Biblical Authority," *Interpretation* 25 (1971), pp. 24–40; and his several summary statements, "Biblical Theology," "Revelation in History," and "Scripture, Authority of," in *IDB Suppl.* 1976, pp. 104–11, pp. 746–49, pp. 794–97. Barr's position has been sharply criticized by Wells, *op. cit.* I do not believe that Wells offers any viable alternative, but he does make clear that Barr's position is not an adequate one for constructive work, though his criticism surely has been needed.

[12]James Barr, "Story and History in Biblical Theology," JR 56 (1976), pp.1–17, now reprinted in *The Scope and Authority of the Bible*, Explorations in Theology 7 (London: SCM Press, 1980) as chapter 1. Zimmerli himself would agree with the character of story: "Narrative is the only possible speech form not only in passages that look back at Yahweh's past self-manifestation, but also in prophetic proclamation that alludes to coming divine manifestation." That claim is not far from the mature summary of Wright, *The Old Testament and Theology* (New York: Harper and Row, 1969), chapter 2. Perhaps even Barr's conclusion approaches this same judgment, albeit by avoiding the troublesome word "history."

[13]James Robinson, "The Historicality of Biblical Language," *The Old Testament and Christian Faith*, ed. Bernhard Anderson (New York: Harper and Row, 1963), pp. 124–158, has made a helpful distinction

between "historicality" and "historicity." On Zimmerli's rejection of Bultmann, see Robinson, "Revelation as Word and as History," *Theology as History*, ed. Robinson and Cobb (New York: Harper and Row, 1967), p. 44, 130.

[14]See the comment of Hans-Joachim Kraus, *Die Biblische Theologie* 333, n. 41, that Zimmerli intends to refute the "gnostic-existential categories of understanding."

[15]Childs, *Introduction*, p. 370.

[16]E.g., *Old Testament Theology in Outline*, pp. 21–27. In his preface (p. 11), Zimmerli acknowledges that von Rad's theology has been his constant dialogue partner, both in agreement and disagreement.

[17]The general problem of history and revelation has generated an enormous literature. In addition to the article by Rendtorff cited in n. 8, "The Concept of Revelation in Ancient Israel," pp. 23–53, to which Zimmerli responded in 1962, see the general review by James Robinson, "Revelation as Word and as History," especially pp. 42–62, the important refinement of Rolf Knierim, "Offenbarung im Alten Testament." *Probleme Biblischer Theologie*, ed. Hans Walter Wolff (München: Chr. Kaiser Verlag, 1971), pp. 206–35, and the most helpful summary of A. H. J. Gunneweg, *Understanding the Old Testament* (Philadelphia: Westminster, 1978), pp. 189–209. Specifically Gunneweg shows that Zimmerli has guarded himself from the extreme claims of Rendtorff concerning the juxtaposition of history and revelation. Zimmerli has regularly insisted that the word itself is a disclosure, not because of the nature of language in general, but because of *who* speaks this word and *what* is said. See also the summary comment of Moltmann, *op. cit.*, pp. 112–116.

[18]M. Douglas Meeks, *Origins of the Theology of Hope* (Philadelphia: Fortress Press, 1974), p. 68, but see p. 90, n. 34.

[19]Zimmerli, *Man and His Hope in the Old Testament* SBT 20[2] (Naperville: Alec R. Allenson, n.d.) but the German publication is from 1968. See also *Old Testament Theology in Outline,* pp.167–240 and especially paragraph 23, and *The Old Testament and the World* (Atlanta: John Knox Press, 1976), chapter 10.

[20]Zimmerli, "Das zweite Gebot," reprinted in *Gottes Offenbarung*, pp. 234–238, and *Old Testament Theology in Outline,* pp. 120–24. The parenthetical title for Zimmerli's English version includes "and against Misusing the Name of God."

[21]von Rad, *Old Testament Theology I*, pp. 212–219.

[22]The two-sidedness of *announcement* and *polemic* is of course fully appreciated by Zimmerli: "In all the passages, where the formula of self-introduction appears in its short two-part form, Yahweh's self-exaltation is spoken as a delimitation over against potential rival gods." This two-sidedness with reference to the name permits a linkage to the work of Ricoeur. In *Freud and Philosophy* as well as *The Conflict of Interpretations*

Ricoeur has urged that we must practice two hermeneutics, one which is an act of suspicion which demystifies and demythologizes, and the other which is an act of affirmation and symbolization. The formulae by Zimmerli provide a biblical base for this two-sidedness. The self-disclosure of the name of Yahweh not only celebrates Yahweh but delegitimates every false claimant. This is more popularly summarized by Ricoeur in his two articles now printed in *The Philosophy of Paul Ricoeur*, ed. by Charles E. Reagen and David Stewart (Boston: Beacon Press, 1978). The critical act is characterized in "The Critique of Religion," pp. 213–22, and the confessional counterpart in "The Language of Faith," pp. 223–38. In both cases the ground is the naming of the name.

I would not want to press the links to Ricoeur too far, but I observe the following: Zimmerli speaks of "rethinking" (umdenkende) after the failure of 587. In his essay, "Biblical Hermeneutics," *Semeia* 4 (1975) 31, Ricoeur follows Mary Hesse in speaking of the poetic approach as a means of "redescribing reality." Perhaps the notions of *rethinking* in Zimmerli (applied to Ezekiel 40—48) and *redescribing* in Ricoeur are not so very different. Both seek to find a way for language to form a newness after the complete failure of what is old. The linkage is that Zimmerli enquires into the *theological substance* of such an act and Ricoeur pays attention to the *function of language* in such a possibility.

²³See Zimmerli's exposition of the passage, *I Mose 1-11* (Zürich: Zwingli Verlag, 1943), pp. 188–206. Zimmerli, *Old Testament Theology in Outline*, pp. 19–21, begins his theological statement with "God's free revelation" which is premised in Yahweh's "spontaneity" in announcing himself. Zimmerli shows that he intends these articles to be the foundation for his entire theological statement.

²⁴See Knierim, *op. cit.*, pp. 223–224, on the cruciality of the name. Zimmerli asserts that everything else Yahweh has to disclose is an "amplification" of that fundamental statement.

I Am Yahweh

¹Similarly, for example, Holzinger (KHK); Baentsch (HK); Gressmann (SAT²); Köhler, *ThR* NF 1 (1929), p. 179.

²Albrecht Alt, "The Origins of Israelite Law," in *Essays on Old Testament History and Religion*, trans. R. A. Wilson (Oxford: Basil Blackwell, 1966), p. 130; Martin Noth, *The Laws in the Pentateuch and Other Studies*, trans. D. R. AP-Thomas (Philadelphia: Fortress, 1966), p. 20, footnote 38.

³Poebel, *Das appositionell bestimmte Pronomen der 1. Person sing. in den westsemitischen Inschriften und im Alten Testament* (1932).

⁴As a secular analogy cf. the '*ny ywsp* of Genesis 45:3, in which Joseph discloses his personal secret to his brothers.

[5]Albrecht Alt, *Essays on Old Testament History and Religion*, p. 130: "covenant promise."

[6]Cf. Bergsträsser's discussion of Poebel's study, OLZ 37 (1934), pp. 173 f. Cf. also Alt, *Origins of Israelite Law*, p. 130, footnote 121.

[7]Gerhard von Rad, *Studies in Deuteronomy*, trans. David Stalker (London: SCM, 1953), pp. 25 ff.

[8]From this perspective Leviticus 17 does not follow the Holiness Code.

[9]Klostermann's translation in *Der Pentateuch* (1893), "I Yahweh," does not adequately account for the conventions of nominal clauses in Hebrew.

[10]We will shortly speak of the secondary form-critical alteration.

[11]To that extent this expanded formula expresses Israel's particular covenant experience. However, this is already implicit in the short formula according to its Old Testament understanding. Köhler's assertion that "the name of God in prayer and revelation is always accompanied by an addendum establishing the relationship between deity and worshiper" does not always hold true in the Holiness Code (Köhler, *ThR*, NF 1 [1929], p. 179).

[12]The singular form *'lhyk* found in the Decalogue does not occur in the Holiness Code.

[13]Cf. also Lev. 11:45. Klostermann already recognized (*ThR* NF 1 1929, p. 377) that not only Exodus 6:6–8, but also Exodus 12:12b; 29:28–46; 31:13 ff.; Lev. 11:43–45; Num. 3:12 f.; 10:8–10; 15:38–41 employ the formula of self-introduction in a style similar to that of the Holiness Code. We need not discuss here whether his assertion is correct that "Leviticus 18—26 only contains fragments of a comprehensive legal code, individual parts of which we also find in Exodus and Numbers" (p. 378).

[14]The overall structure of Leviticus 22:32 f. sooner suggests the first rendering.

[15]From this perspective we can, of course, ask whether the formula *'ny yhwh 'lhykm* has not also undergone an accent displacement in the course of this formal alteration. I think the unaffected interchange of *'ny yhwh* and *'ny yhwh 'lhykm* speaks against this as far as the Holiness Code is concerned. The statement in Psalm 50:7, discussed in part 6, will be of decisive importance for the Old Testament understanding of the Decalogue preamble.

[16]Jeremiah 24:7 has combined the two possibilities in a kind of awkward addition: *wntty lhm lb ld't 'ty ky 'ny yhwh*.

[17]Ezek. 5:15, 17; 17:21; 21:22; (23:34); 24:14; (26:5); 30:12; 34:24 or 17:24; 22:14; 36:36.

[18]The most preferable seems to be Klostermann's rendering "I Yahweh" (cf. footnote 9). Cf. also the employment of the formula of

self-introduction in Exodus 12:12. Verses 13 and 45 are noteworthy in Numbers 3.

[19]This alludes back to Genesis 17:1, where Yahweh's speech begins with the formula of self-introduction *'ny 'l šdy*.

[20]The *zr' byt y'qb* can really hardly be considered as such; cf. further footnote 24.

[21]Is there beyond this yet another actualization directed to Ezekiel's own time? The anti-Egyptian polemic in the book of Ezekiel is of central importance; cf. for example chapter 23.

[22]According to Exodus 31:18a and 34:29, which mention the commandments, P apparently also knows about the Decalogue. Where, however, does he integrate the conveyance of the Decalogue into the narrative context?

[23]20:44; also the *lm'n šmy* in vss. 9, 14, 22.

[24]The absence of any of the customary talk about the land sworn to the fathers pointedly underscores the exclusion of the patriarchal tradition.

[25]In the same chapter Ezekiel 20:19 also shows us the preambular form familiar from the Decalogue. Cf. also Lev. 18:4.

[26]Also Exod. 31:13. In the majority of the cases the formula of self-introduction has been added asyndetically. This is always the case when the short form of the formula appears. The expanded form is variously added in a looser style with *ky*. *ky'ny yhwh 'lhykm* (*'lhym*) appears in 24:22; 25:17; 26:1, 44. *ky 'ny yhwh mqdšw* (*mqdšm*) appears in 21:15, 23; 22:16. The formula appears not only as an addendum to sentences spoken in Yahweh's first-person discourses, but also (cf. 19:23–25) as the conclusion of a speech that mentions Yahweh in the third person. This shows that the commandment sentences are not constructed with an eye primarily on the concluding formula of self-introduction; we encounter here rather a secondary employment (in the context of certain commandment recitations?).

[27]Cf. also the introductions in 19:1 f.; 20:1 f.; they are limited to the circle of priests in 21:1, 17; 22:1. To be sure, the introductory formula of self-introduction is missing here.

[28]We encounter it more frequently above all in the book of Exodus (in addition to the Priestly passages already mentioned [6:7 and 29:46], cf. also the Priestly and Yahwistic passages 7:5, 17; 8:18; 10:2; 14:4, 18; 16:12; 31:13) and further in Deuteronomy 29:5; 1 Kings 20:13, 28; Jeremiah 24:7; Joel 2:27; 4:17. We have already spoken about Ezekiel, and we will speak later about Deutero-Isaiah. I hope to examine the statement of recognition at another time [see the following two articles].

[29]Concerning the distribution of *'ny* and *'nky*, the Priestly circle (Ezek., Holiness Code, P) again sharply distinguishes itself by its exclusive use of *'ny* (aside from the formula of self-introduction, only in 36:28 does Ezekiel use *'nky*; this shows it to be a secondary usage). On the other hand,

the Elohist uses only *'nky* in passages we can recognize as containing the self-introductory formula (similar to Deuteronomy, which uses *'ny* only in 12:30, a passage which is probably also only a secondary addendum). The remaining writings show us the customary loose employment; concerning the Yahwist, cf. the juxtaposition of Gen. 15:7 and 26:24; concerning Deutero-Isaiah, cf. juxtaposition within the same verse, 45:12; cf. also Hos. 5:14; Jer. 24:7; Judg. 6:8–10.

[30]Gressmann, *AOT*[2], pp. 266 f.

[31]Schmidtke, *Asarhaddons Statthalterschaft in Babylonien und seine Thronbesteigung in Assyrien 681 v. Chr.* (1916), pp. 119 f.; cf. Gressmann, *AOT*[2], p. 282; Pritchard, *ANET* (1950), p. 450.

[32]*Die Welt des Orients* I 5 (1950), p. 402.

[33]*Studies in Old Testament Prophecy*, ed. H. H. Rowley (1950), pp. 103 ff.

[34]Concerning the interrogative form of the formula of self-introduction, cf. the Old Testament parallel Isa. 45:21: "Am I not Yahweh, and there is no other god besides me."

[35]Hempel, in *Die althebräische Literatur* (1930), p. 32, refers to the genre-historical relationship between this divine self-praise and the secular boasting song. Ed. Norden, *Agnostos Theos* (1923), pp. 177–239, and Ed. Schweizer, *Ego eimi* (1939), pp. 12–14, have collected a rich source of material (though without making the distinctions we have) for the religio-historical comparison of the formula of self-introduction. S. Schott, *Myth und Mythenbildung im alten Ägypten* (1945), p. 131 f., discusses a special employment within the context of the ancient Egyptian transfiguration of the dead king, who inserts himself into the myth by speaking the formula of self-introduction. We cannot discuss here the secular usage of the formula in royal inscriptions. According to Mowinckel ("Die vorderasiatischen Königs- und Fürsteninschriften," in *Eucharisterion für H. Gunkel* I (1923), p. 315) the elements of self-glorification in these inscriptions are secondarily influenced by the hymn of the votive inscription. Similarly Gressmann, cf. the following footnote.

[36]Gressmann, *ZAW* 34 (1914), pp. 286 f., deals specifically with the formula of self-introduction as an epiphany formula that should be understood within the original context of polytheism; Köhler, *Deutero-Isaiah*, BZAW 37 (1923), pp. 121 f., deals with the self-predication in Deutero-Isaiah.

[37]Concerning a further participial supplement, cf. 45:19, used in the statement of recognition in 49:26.

[38]*'ny hw'* in 41:4; 43:10; 48:12 (cf. also 44:6); also 51:12 and the secondary Deutero-Isaiah passage 52:6.

[39]45:5–7, 18–19 has apparently undergone some sort of expansion, and we find a repeated exposition of the formula of self-introduction. This may also be the case in Exodus 29:46; Leviticus 11:44 f.; 22:32–33 within the

context of the Priestly statements. The formula of self-introduction has a natural tendency toward expansion and fullness.

[40]What Begrich, *Studien zu Deuterojesaja* (1938), pp. 44 f., has called a disputation statement in 44:24–28 is formally a statement of Yahweh's pure hymnic self-predication. The formula of self-introduction has been augmented by nine participial predications; from the fourth onward they are continued by means of a finite verb. Concerning the participial style, cf. Norden, *Agnostos Theos*, pp. 201 ff.

[41]Concerning the placement of the statement of recognition within the oracular supplication answer, cf. Begrich, *Deuterojesaja*, pp. 10 f.

[42]Cf. 45:6, 18; in a disrupted form also in 45:22; 46:9.

[43]41:10 shows us the continuation without the *yhwh*.

[44]In contrast, the divine name *yhwh ṣb'wt* appears frequently in the third person: *yhwh ṣb'wt šmw;* 47:4; 48:2; 51:15; 54:5. A glance at Jeremiah 10:16; 31:35; 32:18; 46:18; 48:15; 50:34; 51:19, 57; Amos 4:13; 5:27 suggests this is a fixed formula that resists any modification into first person.

[45]Isaiah 27:3 does not reflect the formula of self-introduction to any great degree.

[46]Does the commandment formulation here allude to the style of the oracular supplication answer (*'l tyr'*)?

[47]*Le décalogue* (1927), pp. 125, 129 f.

[48]Mowinckel, *Le décalogue*, pp. 125 f.; Gerhard von Rad, *The Problem of the Hexateuch and Other Essays*, trans. E. W. Trueman Dicken (New York: McGraw Hill, 1966), pp. 21 ff.; cf. also Gunkel, *Die Psalmen* (1926) concerning this passage.

[49]Weiser's translation (ATD), "I, the Lord, am your God," is linguistically impossible. [In the meantime Weiser has corrected this (5th edition): "I am the Lord, your God." Arthur Weiser, *The Psalms, A Commentary,* trans. Herbert Hartwell (Philadelphia: Westminster, 1962).]

[50]Gunkel's alterations are completely arbitrary (*Die Psalmen*).

[51]The syndetic connection shows that the divine word of the Mara pericope is also a secondary formation; the content and stylistic break inside Exodus 15:26 also suggests this (the change from "he" to Yahweh's "I"-form). This says nothing about the age and significance of the formula *'ny yhwh rp'k*. It may very well have had its own particular *Sitz im Leben*, but one will hardly be able to determine exactly where without a thorough investigation into the verb *rp'*.

[52]Cf. *Festschrift Bertholet* (1950), pp. 550 ff.

[53]*Eucharisterion für Gunkel* I (1923), p. 90.

[54]Cf. also Deut. 33:2 ff.

[55]*Le décalogue,* pp. 140 f. "The epiphany originally took place with a view to the covenant and the promise of blessing, and not with a view to a proclamation of the law. This latter element, as regards the cultic epiphany,

is secondary . . . . The cult of the people of ancient Israel was thus not a cult of the word, neither in the sense of predication nor of exhortation."

[56]Cf. von Rad's sensible observations in "Verkündigung und Forschung," Theologischer Jahresbericht (1947/48), pp. 188 f.

[57]Hempel attempts to comprehend these elements in a different way, *Die althebräische Literatur*, p. 32.

[58]The closest form-critical parallel would probably be found in the Hammurabi Code, which belongs in the context of royal inscriptions in which the king, not the deity, is associated with the formula of self-introduction. Cf. footnote 35.

Knowledge of God According to the Book of Ezekiel

[1]Among previous investigations cf. J. Hänel, *Das Erkennen Gottes bei den Schriftpropheten*, BWAT 4 (1923), who examines the ways the prophets believed they received the revelation. S. Mowinckel, *Die Erkenntnis Gottes bei den alttestamentlichen Propheten* (1941), also looks first at the experiential form of the way the prophet received the word; however, he then goes on to sketch the content of prophetic knowledge of God. G. J. Botterweck's work, *Gott erkennen im Sprachgebrauch des Alten Testamentes*, BBB 2 (1951), deals with the entire Old Testament and is conducted as a conceptual investigation. W. Reiss, in his essay "Gott nicht kennen im Alten Testament," ZAW 58 (1940/41), pp. 70–98, offers a rather general classification of statements concerned with failure to know God. H. W. Wolff examines Hosea's understanding of knowledge of God, in "Wissen um Gott bei Hosea als Urform von Theologie," Ev. Theol 12 (1952/53), pp. 533-52; reprinted in his *Gesammelte Studien*, ThB 22 (München: 1973[2]), pp. 182–205. Cf. also R. Bultmann's article *gignóskein* in Kittel's *Theological Dictionary of the New Testament*.

[2]Mandelkern lists the infinitive *d't* separately, a term that stabilized into an independent substantive; it is missing in Ezekiel (Solomon Mandelkern, *Veteris Testamenti Concordantiae Hebraicae atque Chaldaicae* [Graz: Akademische Druck u. Verlagsanstalt, 1955]). Of the 91 occurrences of this *d't*, not less that 58 are found within the limited circle of the wisdom books (Proverbs, Job, and Ecclesiastes). We encounter the genuine verbal infinitive in Ezekiel 20:12, 20; 38:16.

[3]And an additional 4 occurrences for the substantive infinitive. Only about one-fourth of the 68 occurrences of the Qal involve knowledge of Yahweh.

[4]And an additional 10 occurrences for the substantive infinitive. In the 62 occurrences of the Qal, God is the object of knowledge a total of 5 times.

[5]The passages are: 6:7, 13, 14; 7:4, 27; 11:10, 12; 12:15, 16, 20; 13:9, 14, 21, 23; 14:8; 15:7; 16:62; 20:26, 38, 42, 44; 22:16; 23:49; 24:24, 27; 25:7, 9, 11, 17; 26:6; 28:22, 23, 24; 29:6, 9, 16, 21; 30:8, 19, 25, 26; 32:15; 33:29;

144   I AM YAHWEH

34:27; 35:4, 9, 15; 36:11, 23, 38; 37:6, 13; 38:23; 39:6. *'dny* is added 5 times in the Masoretic Text (13:9; 23:49; 28:24; 29:16 (*wyd'tm-wyd'w ky 'ny 'dny yhwh*); *ky* is once replaced by *'šr* (*lm'n 'šr yd' w šr 'ny yhwh*, 20:26).

[6]5:13; 6:13; 17:21, 24; 21:10; 22:22; 35:12; 36:36; 37:14. Cf. also footnote 10.

[7]20:20; 28:26; 39:22, 28. This would also include the adjectival expansion in 39:7: "And the nations shall know that I am Yahweh, the Holy One in Israel."

[8]7:9; 20:12; 37:28.

[9]34:30: "And they shall know that I, Yahweh, am with them."

[10]G[B] leads to the shorter textual version: "and they shall know that I, Yahweh, have spoken." Accordingly, one may add the passage in footnote 6.

[11]In addition to 14:23 we may also include the passages 2:5; 25:14; 33:33; 38:16 (cf. footnote 20).

[12]In the remaining passages, Yahweh is the subject of recognition in 11:5 and 37:3. 10:20; 17:12; 28:19; 32:9 all speak in a general fashion about human knowledge. 19:7 and 38:14 are perhaps corrupted texts that originally did not contain the verb *yd'*.

[13]This accusative formulation also occurs in 25:14 and 38:16 in a statement of recognition formed with *yd'*; cf. also footnotes 22 and 49 below.

[14]Certainly the prophet himself was not the only one who worked on the book of Ezekiel. One should, however, totally agree with Rowley; in his survey of recent scholarship on the book of Ezekiel. *The Book of Ezekiel in Modern Study*, Bulletin of the John Rylands Library 36 (1953), pp. 166 f., he insists that the measure of editorial additions should not be exaggerated and that even where redaction is discernible, it does not drift very far from Ezekiel himself. Even though the old view of Ezekiel's literary unity has been superceded, the book cannot even marginally be compared with the book of Isaiah, nor with the book of Jeremiah, as regards the kind of editorial reworking and addenda we encounter. This justifies our examining the book of Ezekiel as a coherent whole in what follows and only occasionally dealing with the question of primary or secondary literary material. From the perspective of the recognition process, the book's statements are astonishingly homogeneous and lie along a completely different line than those of the other prophetic books.

[15]Concerning the text, cf. BHK[3]. In what follows one should also compare the apparatus of the BHK[3] with any silently undertaken textual corrections.

[16]We will have to discuss this formulation of the recognition content and its relationship to knowledge of Yahweh in a later context.

[17]Cf., e.g., 6:8–10; 12:16; 14:21–23.

[18]We find an imperfect only in 20:26. Cf. also footnote 19.

[19]Cf. the doubling of the final statement, the use of *lm'n 'šr* instead of the simple *w consecutivum* (only once in Ezekiel), and the use of the imperfect instead of the *perfectum consecutivum* made necessary by this. The second final sentence is also missing in G^B. Its absence creates an unmistakable easing of the contextual meaning.

[20]A statement directed to Gog says: "I will bring you against my land, that the nations may know me, when through you, O Gog, I vindicate my holiness before their eyes." This passage is thrown into relief against the other formulations by the connection with the simple *lm'n* which occurs only here (also *lm'n 'šr* in 20:26) and by the designation of the recognition content by a simple accusative *'wty* (which occurs only here) as compared with differently oriented passages 25:14 (cf. footnote 22 below) and 39:21 (see footnote 13 above). In contrast to 20:26, however, it cannot so easily be separated from the context as a later addition.

[21]Bultmann, *Theological Dictionary of the New Testament*, p. 696 f. Luther's rendering of the formula of recognition, "you will see (experience) that I am the Lord," has properly understood that God does not touch the human being merely in the capacity for intellectual knowledge; God's activity rather seizes and tries to master the entire breadth of life.

[22]In addition to the passage cited in footnote 20 (38:16), we find the same formal expansion of the statement in 5:13 as well. At this point we must also refer to the freer formulation in 25:14. In a threat to Edom the concluding statement of recognition there reads: "And they shall know my vengeance" (*wyd'w 't nqmty*). We see that what we designated as recognition material offered by Yahweh (in 25:17) can virtually be designated as the recognition content itself. To recognize Yahweh means quite literally to recognize his vengeful activity. To recognize Yahweh means to recognize his work. Finally, the comparison of 25:14 and 17 is also instructive in that it shows us that the statement of recognition in 25:14, constructed with a simple accusative object, is basically an abbreviation of a fuller formulation of an objective clause. According to 25:17 the full formulation would read: "'And they shall know that I, Yahweh, exercise vengeance." The statement constructed with the verb *r'h* in 39:21 should also be considered an analogous abbreviation; it can effortlessly be altered into the statement, "and all the nations shall see that I [Yahweh] hold judgment and lay my hand on them." Cf. footnote 13 above.

[23]12:15–16 probably do not belong here since verse 16 begins a new complex.

[24]This is the case in 5:13; 6:13; 12:15; 15:7; 20:42, 44; 25:17; 28:22; 30:8, 25; 33:29; 34:27; 36:23 (?); 37:14; 38:16; 39:28.

[25]Let us once more underscore the parameters of this investigation. In what follows we are not involved in a general examination of "knowledge of God in the Old Testament." We wish rather to investigate what lies behind

the characteristic form of speech dominant in the book of Ezekiel which we designate as the statement of recognition or recognition formula and to inquire into its specific content.

[26]Martin Noth, *Überlieferungsgeschichtliche Studien* I (1943), p. 80, footnote 1, directed against Eissfeldt, HSAT⁴, pp. 535 ff. Cf. also Jepsen, *Die Quellen des Königsbuches* (1953), p. 78.

[27]Let us refer here to the alteration in the form of the statement of recognition (you singular [shall know] . . . you [plural] shall know), an alteration not really explained by the textual context; the Greek translation already balances this out. We observe a similar inconsistency in the formulation of the statement of recognition in the book of Ezekiel as well, an inconsistency again not immediately illuminated by the context; in Ezekiel it is still a problem that has not yet been satisfactorily resolved. There also the various versions show a tendency to level the texts.

[28]Concerning specifics, cf. Gerhard von Rad, *Der heilige Krieg im alten Israel*, ATANT 20 (1951).

[29]Cf. also A. Jepsen, *Nabi* (1934), pp. 90 f., who dates the events of 1 Kings 20 during the reign of King Joash of Israel.

[30]Concerning Exodus 6 cf. the exposition in the preceding article, "I Am Yahweh." H. Haag, *Was lehrt die literarische Untersuchung des Ezechiel-Textes*? (1943), pp. 25–27 has justifiably drawn attention to the relationship between Ezekiel and Exodus 6 and offers an extensive discourse on the statement of recognition. As the present study clearly shows, however, the assumption of a direct dependence of Ezekiel on the Priestly writing inadmissibly oversimplifies the problem of tradition. The passages in 1 Kings 20 prompt us to view Ezekiel's use of the statement of recognition within the context of an older prophetic tradition. On the other hand, there can be no doubt that he has been strongly influenced by Priestly content; cf. my analysis of Ezekiel 14:1–11 in ZAW 66 (1954), pp. 1 ff. The real tradition-critical problem as regards the prophecy of Ezekiel and the circle following him is the combination of priestly and prophetic influence.

[31]Verse 8 is a parallel statement of clarification to verse 7 in which two infinitives introduced by *b* try to clarify the means by which Yahweh will bring about recognition. The second infinitive statement does, to be sure, anticipate essentially and unbecomingly the statement Yahweh had reserved for himself (vs. 12). Further, we ought to draw attention to the fine parallelism between *r'h* and *yd'* in verse 6.

[32]Cf. also the form of the doubled concluding statement here. Although this does not repeat the full statement of recognition, it does repeat the "I am Yahweh" found in the strict statement of recognition (expanded by the phrase "your God" that expresses the covenant relationship). See above pp. 33 f.

[33]See below pp. 69 f.

[34]Concerning the form cf. footnote 32.

[35]The uncertainties regarding source determination in the Moses stories prevents us from drawing any certain conclusions. Nontheless, we observe that in the entire Old Testament only in Psalm 46:10 does the strict statement of recognition use *'nky*. Concerning the distribution of *'ny* and *'nky*, cf. above, "I Am Yahweh," footnote 29.

[36]Numbers 16:1*b*, 2*a*α, 12–15, 25–26, 27*b*, 34. In the present text this account is contained within the Korah story.

[37]Gerhard von Rad, *Studies in Deuteronomy*, trans. David Stalker (London: SCM, 1953), pp. 11 ff.

[38]The plural formulation in verses 7–8*a* shows them to be later textual additions.

[39]We can probably recognize this kind of open alteration of the statement of recognition into the imperative form in Psalms 46:10; 103:2; (4:3).

[40]Deuteronomy 4:35 (*'yn 'wd mlbdw*) and 39 (*'yn 'wd*) clearly expressed the accent of exclusivism found in this formulation.

[41]Concerning Elijah's prayer in 1 Kings 18:37, which should also be mentioned here, see below p. 62. The appearance of the Deuteronomic formulation in the pre-Deuteronomic Elijah and Isaiah legends is probably of some significance for the evaluation of the origin of Deuteronomic language.

[42]Concerning the more freely formulated statement of recognition in Joshua's Deuteronomistic farewell speech in Joshua 23:14, see below, p. 61.

[43]Joshua 23:14 adds: "know in your hearts and souls." Cf. also Deut. 8:5 *wyd't 'm lbbk*.

[44]J. Begrich, "Das priesterliche Heilsorakel," ZAW 52 (1934), pp. 81–92; *Studien zu Deuterojesaja*, BWANT IV 25 (1938), pp. 6–19.

[45]The strict statement of recognition has been dismantled at the end to the extent that the *'ny yhwh* is pushed into its own concluding nominal clause, and now appears as an independent formula of self-introduction. Cf. above, pp. 17-22.

[46]Perhaps this is the best reading (following Begrich, *Studien zu Deuterojesaja*, p. 41) instead of the obscure second person plural offered by the Masoretic Text.

[47]In verse 12 we then find only the stereotyped refrain that does not belong to the specific content of the strophe. The *'lhym* in verse 11 naturally owes its existence to the Elohistic redaction of the "Elohistic Psalter" and should be replaced by the original *yhwh*.

[48]We find this manner of expression twice in the related word of promise in Jeremiah 31:34: "And no longer shall each man teach his neighbor and each his brother, saying, 'Know Yahweh,' for they shall all know me, from the least of them to the greatest." Cf. further Jer. 4:22; (5:4, 5; 8:7); 9:2, 5, 23; 22:16; Hos. 2:22; 5:4; 6:3; 8:2; 13:4; also Hab. 2:14. In

Hosea we never encounter the "strict statement of recognition" (see below, chapter 5b) that predominates in Ezekiel, and in Jeremiah we find it only in the combined form we are now discussing (24:7). Jeremiah 16:21, the concluding statement of 16:19–21 that we will mention next, is doubtlessly post-Deutero-Isaian. Cf. W. Rudolph, *Jeremia* (1947).

⁴⁹We find the simple accusative formulation only in 38:16 in the concluding statement to what is likely a secondary textual addition, 38:14–16. Concerning the accusative formulations in 25:14 and 39:21 cf. footnote 22. Concerning 38:16 cf. also footnote 20.

⁵⁰The prayer in 1 Kings 8:43, in which the first half of the verse also speaks about recognizing Yahweh's name, was already mentioned in the context of the Deuteronomistic statements (p. 53).

⁵¹K. Marti, "Der Zweifel an der prophetischen Sendung Sacharjas," *Festschrift J. Wellhausen*, BZAW 27 (1914), pp. 297 ff.

⁵²In 2:13, 15 the statement is given in the form of a first-person speech by Yahweh. 4:9 and 6:15 describe the rebuilding of the temple as being comprehensible only as Yahweh's merciful deed; 4:9 names Zerubbabel as the human agent of this reconstruction.

⁵³The divine word accompanied by a concluding statement of recognition appears to echo all the way into the wisdom teaching of the book of Job; it is now a form emptied for the most part of its original content that acts as a solemn conclusion to statements wishing to announce emphatically some divine activity. This is apparently how we should understand the doubled *wyd't* near the end of the first speech of Eliphas (5:24 f.) and the concluding line of Job's speech in chapter 19 (vs. 29b: "that you may know there is a judgment"). We find the last biblical descendants of the form of divine saying accompanied by a concluding statement of recognition in the Revelation of John. It appears clearly in the threat against the woman Jezebel within the speech to the congregation of Thyatira; in the threat—statement of recognition sequence (directed to the congregations) we read: "Behold, I will throw her on a sickbed, and those who commit adultery with her I will throw into great tribulation, unless they repent of her doings; and I will strike her children dead. And all the churches shall know that I am he who searches mind and heart, and I will give to each of you as your works deserve" (Rev. 2:22 f.). The form of the prophetic saying is astonishingly well preserved here. It is more extensively dismantled in 3:9, significantly again in a threat against the people from Satan's synagogue; it is dismantled to the extent that the recognition is no longer the result of divine activity but is rather announced directly by the divine word as a coming event: "Behold, I will make them come and bow down before your feet, and know that I have loved you." The influence of Isaiah 49:23 is clearly discernable here.

⁵⁴We should also interpret Jeremiah 24:7 from this perspecive, where the object clause appears as the interpretation of the accusative statement

that stands first. As a result, the object clause occurs in an abbreviated form without an intentionally preceding statement of a specific divine action.

[55]Cf. further the prayer formulations in Pss. 59:13; 83:18; 109:27; (9:20; 67:2).

[56]More concerning this in chapter 7.

[57]Significantly, we do not find a recognition formula in the brief priestly remark in 1:17.

[58]The line of demarcation between the priestly and prophetic supplication answer has still not been determined. Is the priest concerned only with inquiries from individuals and with their personal concerns, while beyond that (the Elijah and Elisha stories show that the prophet can also be involved with the concerns of individuals) the prophet is also involved with the concerns of Israel, the people of Yahweh, for example in holy war? Or are the mutual spheres indistinguishable? This question involves, among other things, the much discussed problems of cult prophecy. How were the various spheres of prophetic and priestly mediation of divine messages ultimately differentiated? Where do the spheres overlap and where are they separate? Cf. footnote 76.

[59]2 Chronicles 33:13 also lets the supplication answer follow immediately upon Manasseh's prayer without it being announced beforehand by Yahweh's emissary. Although recognition emerges from this, its consequences are not developed further. "He prayed to him, and God received his entreaty and heard his supplication and brought him again to Jerusalem into his kingdom. Then Manasseh knew Yahweh was God."

[60]H. Gunkel, *Die Psalmen* (1926), p. 22; F. Küchler, "Das priesterliche Orakel in Israel und Juda," *Festschrift W. von Baudissin*, BZAW 33 (1918), pp. 285–301; H. Gunkel-J. Begrich, *Einleitung in die Psalmen* (1933), pp. 243 ff.; J. Begrich (see footnote 44).

[61]Martin Noth, "Die Vergegenwärtigung des Alten Testamentes in der Verkündigung," Ev. Theol. 12 (1952/53), pp. 6 –17.

[62]Mic. 6:5: "O my people, remember what Balak king of Moab devised, and what Balaam the son of Beor answered him, and what happened from Shittim to Gilgal, that you may know the saving acts of Yahweh" (*lm'n d't ṣdqwt yhwh*). Within this context we can compare the accusative formulation that deviates formally somewhat. Cf. also footnote 22.

[63]One can ask whether this is not the place where the entire priestly knowledge of the Holy—a knowledge initially formulated and taught in a completely timeless fashion—finds its theological integration. Concerning this priestly *d't*, cf. Begrich, "Die priesterliche Tora," *Werden und wesen des Alten Testamentes* ed. J. Hempel, BZAW 66 (1936), pp. 63–88; R. Rendtorff, *Die Gesetze in der Priesterschrift*, FRLANT 44 (1954). In his examination of Hosea's statements (cf. footnote 1), H. W. Wolff tries to show that within the understanding of *d't* presupposed by Hosea a

familiarity both with the historical Credo and with Yahweh's legal claims are intertwined. Wolff's results thus touch on the observations made above, though without addressing the problem of form as regards the various statements of recognition. In the book of Ezekiel one finds the customary speech of the priestly *d't* touched upon in the *hiphil* formulation of 22:26: "Her priests have not taught knowledge (*hwdy'w* denom. from *d't*?) of the difference between the clean and the unclean"; parallel 44:23. Against the background of these statements we have to ask seriously whether Yahweh's commission to the prophet—"Son of man, make known to Jerusalem her abominations (*hwd'*)." 16:2, correspondingly 20:4; 22:2— does not represent a polemical, prophetic antithesis against the usual priestly teaching.

[64]We must once again emphasize that we are examining the structure of the recognition formulation as found in Ezekiel, a formulation that expresses the recognition content in an object clause and is related to its context in a quite characteristic fashion. We are not examining as such the Hosean-Jeremianic statements of recognition with their simple accusative designation of recognition content. It could appear that the imperative formulation assumes a different position there. In Jeremiah 31:34 the teaching of knowledge — one person says to another: know Yahweh (*d'w 't yhwh*)—appears to be the characteristic posture of the covenant member in the Sinai Covenant. Nevertheless, one would still need to examine to what extent the form we are now treating indeed influenced those statements; cf. also the previous footnote.

[65]Concerning the accusative formulations in Ezekiel cf. footnotes 20 and 22.

[66]Cf. also Joseph's speech in verses 18–20, particularly the formulation in verse 20: "And bring your youngest brother to me; so your words will be verified, and you shall not die." Instead of the subjective *wyd'ty* we find here the objective formulation *wy'mnw dbrykm*.

[67]Genesis 22:1 uses the verb *nsh*. Cf. the combination of *nsh* and *yd'* in Deuteronomy 8:2, which speaks of the "testing" in the wilderness: *lnstk ld't 't 'šr blbbk*.

[68]In Judges 6:39 the verb *nsh* is used to describe Gideon's action.

[69]Note the alternative character of the statement and the expression drawn from the milieu of holy war: "Yahweh has given them into our hand." The sign takes the place here of the propetic word of 1 Kings 20:13, 28. Since certainty obtains here, the fate of the Philistines can be formulated in a perfective statement. The statement's end position also corresponds to the structure of the prophetic saying.

[70]Concerning the combination of *wz't lkm h'wt* with the statement of recognition, cf. Jeremiah 44:29 (28) as an example from prophetic sayings. Cf. also C. Keller's monography, *Das Wort OTH als Offenbarungszeichen Gottes* (1946); Keller quite rightly observes that the most frequently

mentioned goal of divine signs is "knowledge."

[71]"For how shall it be known (*bmh yiwwāḍa' 'pw'*) that I have found favor in thy sight, I and thy people? Is it not in thy going with us?" (*blktk 'mnw*). We also encounter this turn of phrase within personal relationships. In 2 Samuel 14:22 Joab says to David: "Today your servant knows that I have found favor in your sight, my lord the king, in that the king has granted the request of his servant." Does Judges 17 also belong in this context of statements in which favor is recognized by a specific external sign? The Ephraimite Micah hears his mother's curse on the thief who steals her money; he quickly consecrates the stolen money to a graven divine image; the mother then follows the curse with a blessing for her son. Micah subsequently wins over a Levite to perform priestly service to the shrine. Does Micah utter the statement of relief in 17:13 in view of the threat of the curse? "Now I know (*'th yd'ty*) that Yahweh will prosper me, because I have a Levite as priest." The sending of a Levite convinces him that the divine curse has been lifted. The event carries for him the weight of divine judgment.

[72]This also shows us a parallel to the conclusion of the angel's speech to the shepherds in Luke 2:12: "And this will be a sign for you . . . ." Here, too, the sign is more than merely a signpost. The low status of the child in the manger carries the meaning of a sign that contrasts what is actually expected (concerning this contrast cf. Zech. 9:9).

[73]Isaiah's granting to King Ahaz the freedom to decipher the sign in its specifics is to be considered a special show of favor. In Daniel 4:14, 22, 29; 5:21 the authoritative interpreter of dreams has replaced the prophet.

[74]As far as we can determine, the Old Testament lacks the kind of refined omina-science that tries to determine a number of differentiated possibilities; A. Ungnad, *Die Religion der Babylonier und Assyrer* (1921), offers examples of such omina-texts from the Fertile Crescent. Cf. also Keller, *Das Wort OTH*, pp. 81 ff.

[75]Gerhard von Rad, *Heiliger Krieg*, pp. 7 ff.

[76]Cf. particularly the priest's administration of the lots (Deut. 33:8). The throwing of the urim and thummin ("oracle and truth")—however this may have been carried out—could decide between alternative questions. "Come hither, all you leaders of the people; and know and see (*d'w wr'w*) how (through whom?) this sin has arisen today," Saul calls to the people before the guilty party is determined through urim and thummin in a series of alternatively deciding lots (1 Sam. 14:38). No priest is mentioned here. Should we silently supply him, or does the king himself function here as a priest? Is Judges 18:5 also a reference to the sacred lots? The Danites say to the priest Micah, "Inquire of God, we pray thee, that we may know (*wnd'h*) whether the journey on which we are setting out will succeed." In any case, this is also a matter of a yes-no question. Of the two passages cited, the first deals with the clarification of a question of guilt, the second with an inquiry

concerning a tribal undertaking. This juxtaposition illuminates once more the difficulty we encounter in differentiating the spheres of priestly and prophetic activity (see footnote 58).

[77]Cf. footnote 63.

[78]Cf. footnote 2.

[79]This is a significant distinction over against the modern understanding of "decision" that places it exclusively within the freedom of the subject.

[80]Concerning the only exception (38:16), see footnotes 20 and 49.

[81]Because Jeremiah 24:7 combined the two possibilities of formulation, we also considered it to be a more precise formulation expressing a new content. See above, pp. 57-58.

[82]Cf. the free alteration within the statement of recognition in Jeremiah 16:21, a secondary passage: "They shall know that my name is Yahweh."

[83]We clearly recognize the usage of this apparently manufactured name in the ancient Egyptian myth of Isis and Ra. G. Roeder, *Urkunden zur Religion des alten Ägypten* (1923), pp. 138–141.

[84]Neither does the singular explanation of Yahweh's name in Exodus 3:14 suggest this.

[85]Concerning this element, cf. B. Gemser, "The Importance of the Motive Clause in Old Testament Law," *Congress Volume Copenhagen* (1953), VT Suppl. 1, pp. 50–66.

[86]In the myth of Isis and Ra as well (footnote 83), clever Isis is able to acquire knowledge of the secret name of Ra only by tricking the old god to whisper his name into her ear. This is also the case in the fairy tale Rumpelstiltskin; one can learn the dwarf's name only by eavesdropping during an unguarded moment when he accidentally calls out his own name.

[87]See above, pp. 12 f.

[88]Hans Joachim Kraus' postulation of an official covenant mediator first visible in Moses, should it prove correct, could open up new perspectives. *Worship in Israel*, trans. Geoffrey Buswell (Richmond: John Knox Press, 1966).

[89]Who is speaking in Psalm 46:10? The use of the pronominal form '*nky* here advises against associating this too closely with the priestly and prophetic statements known to us, statements that stand in peculiar agreement by using only '*ny* in the statement of recognition.

[90]Does this tenacious preservation of the statement of self-introduction not also explain the otherwise striking tendency never to change the strict recognition formula from the first into the second or third person? We search in vain for the statement, "Now I know that you are Yahweh," or, "Know, that he is Yahweh." (The Masoretic version of Isaiah 37:20 reads: "That all the kingdoms of the earth may know that you alone art Yahweh." According to the parallel passage in 2 Kings 19:19, the Isaian passage has been corrupted and originally read: " . . . that you, Yahweh, art God, you

alone.") We encounter free formulations in all the passages in which that kind of formulation might easily suggest itself. The simple displacement of the formula of self-introduction within the strict recognition formula would apparently rob the strict statement of recognition of precisely that which it intends: Yahweh's personal self-introduction that can only occur from his mouth. Thus any attempt to understand the strict statement of recognition in Ezekiel and elsewhere from the perspective of a meaning of the name disclosed by Exodus 3:14 is falsely directed from the very beginning; such attempts fail to recognize the mystery that cannot be reduced to a definition—and the irreversible direction of the process of self-introduction. Concerning the criticism of such attempts cf. Haag, *Was lehrt die literarische Untersuchung des Ezekiel-Textes?*, p. 35.

[91]The Amos studies of Würthwein have shown this quite clearly as regards Amos, ZAW 62 (1949/50), especially pp. 40–52. In Ezekiel we can refer to the impressive historical outline in chapter 20.

[92]Concerning Jeremiah 16:21, cf. p. 59.

[93]G. Fohrer, *Die Hauptprobleme des Buches Ezechiel*, BZAW 72 (1952), pp. 135 ff.

[94]Cf. once again footnote 14.

[95]A final section will discuss the inner characteristics.

[96]"Surely the Lord does nothing, without revealing his secret to his servants the prophets" (Amos 3:7). "Who told this long ago? Who declared it of old? Was it not I, Yahweh?" (Isa. 45:21).

[97]Inquiries concerning the criterium of true prophecy encountered in the Law (Deut. 18:32) and in prophecy (Jer. 28:9) make the reference to the coming of the word. A special problem that we can only mention here is the freedom with which the genuine prophet then lets Yahweh, the Lord of all events, set history aright (Jonah, with his insistence on the literal meaning of the divine word, is the questionable figure within prophecy).

[98]LXX gives the text in abbreviated form.

[99]Concerning the correct understanding of "pro me" cf. H. J. Iwand, "Wider den Missbrauch des pro me als methodisches Prinzip in der Theologie," Ev. Theol. 14 (1954), pp. 120–126.

[100]Botterweck (footnote 1), pp. 67 ff. I can only give a brief sketch of the main aspects here. A commentary to the book of Ezekiel that I hope to publish soon will offer a fuller exposition, one which will deal more extensively with individual questions of literary authenticity. [Walther Zimmerli, *A Commentary on the Book of the Prophet Ezekiel: Chapters 1—24*, trans. R. E. Clements (Philadephia: Fortress, 1979).]

[101]One should note that the statement of recognition is completely absent in the formulation of the new sacred order in chapters 40—48. This once again emphatically confirms the clear relationship of the statement with the proclamation of Yahweh's historical activity.

[102]Only scholarship that fails to recognize its healthy limitations will attribute all these statements to post-Ezekiel redaction. The basic material here probably also goes back to Ezekiel, and the redaction has only clarified things somewhat.

[103]Even someone who does acknowledge that the two passages originally come from Ezekiel has to admit that they in any case express the narrative type of speech concerning Yahweh's activity in a fashion corresponding to Ezekiel.

[104]4:6 appears to expect a period of forty years.

[105]I believe a theological examination of such talk about signs and their relevance in the New Testament message is an urgent need within the framework of current existential interpretation of the New Testament. Matthew 12:39 and 1 Corinthians 1:22 would have to receive as much attention as Luke 2:34 and John 2:11; 20:30 (among others).

[106]Cf. my exposition concerning "Verheissung und Erfüllung," Ev. Theol. 12 (1952/3), pp. 34–59 [Probleme alttestamentlicher Hermeneutik, ThB 11, pp. 69–101].

The Word of Divine Self-manifestation

[1]Artur Weiser, The Old Testament: Its Formation and Development, trans. Dorothea M. Barton (New York: Association Press, 1961), pp. 44–50.

[2]Otto Eissfeldt, The Old Testament: An Introduction, trans. Peter R. Ackroyd (New York: Harper and Row, 1965), pp. 76–81.

[3]Joachim Begrich, "Die priesterliche Tora," in Werden und Wesen des alten Testaments: Vorträge, gehalten auf der internationalen Tagung alttestamentlicher Forscher zu Göttingen vom 4.-10. September 1935, ed. Paul Volz, Friedrich Stummer, and Johannes Hempel, BZAW 66 (1936), pp. 63–88.

[4]Hans Walter Wolff, "Die Begründungen der prophetischen Heils- und Unheilssprüche," ZAW 52 (1934), pp. 1–22.

[5]Walther Zimmerli, "Knowledge of God According to the Book of Ezekiel," see above, pp. 29–98. First published in Abhandlungen zur Theologie des Alten und Neuen Testaments 27 (Zurich: Zwingli Verlag, 1954).

[6]Gerhard von Rad, Der heilige Krieg im alten Israel, ATANT 20 (1951).

[7]For example, in the text of 1 Samuel 14:41 f. corrected according to the LXX.

[8]Gerhard von Rad, "The Levitical Sermon in 1 and 2 Chronicles" (1934), in The Problem of the Hexateuch and other Essays, trans. E. U. Trueman Dicken (New York: McGraw Hill, 1966), pp. 267–280. Der Heilige Krieg, pp. 80–81.

⁹Walther Zimmerli, "Knowledge of God," see above, pp. 72–79. I must still support this assertion despite the objection of Th. Sprey in VT 5 (1955), p. 446. Sprey has apparently not understood at all that the whole investigation is not concerned with the statement of recognition in general, but rather with a speech form that is form-critically structured in a quite specific way (namely, as a result clause). Within this context it is particularly a part of symbolic and proof speech.

¹⁰H. W. Wolff, "Die Begründungen der proph. Heils- u. Unheilssprüche" (footnote 4).

¹¹Walther Zimmerli, "I am Yahweh," included in this volume.

¹²Concerning the concept of "historical Credo" cf. Gerhard von Rad, "The Form-Critical Problem of the Hexateuch," in *The Problem of the Hexateuch and Other Essays*, pp. 1 ff.

¹³Karl Elliger, "Das Gesetz Leviticus 18," ZAW 67 (1955), pp. 1–25, especially pp. 23–25. "Ich bin der Herr—euer Gott," in *Theologie als Glaubenswagnis: Festschrift für Karl Heim* (1954), pp. 9–34.

¹⁴To this extent we can comment more precisely on what was said in the article "I am Yahweh" concerning the translation of the preamble to the Decalogue; in the 'nky yhwh 'lyhk the initially independent elements, "I am Yahweh" and "I am your God," have been combined into one formula that has generated the continuing controversy concerning the translation of the introduction to the Decalogue.

¹⁵Concerning this "objective-tangible" understanding of the name in Deuteronomy, cf. for example Oskar Grether, *Name und Wort Gottes im Alten Testament*, BZAW 64 (1934). In the section "Das Deuteronomium und der Schem-Begriff," pp. 31–35, he does, however, speak only about Deuteronomy hypostasizing the *šem* more strongly than do Exodus 23:31 or Isaiah 30:27.

¹⁶In this sense we can speak more precisely about the phrase '*ny yhwh* in the prophets (going beyond what was said in "Ich bin Yahweh," see above, pp. 16–22).

¹⁷W. Zimmerli, "The Knowledge of God," see above, pp. 53–56.

¹⁸Günther Roeder, "Urkunden zur Religion des Alten Ägypten," in *Religiöse Stimmen der Völker*, ed. Walter Otto (1923), pp. 138–141.

¹⁹Hans Bonnet, *Reallexikon der ägyptischen Religionsgeschichte* (1952), p. 502.

²⁰J. B. Pritchard, *Ancient Near Eastern Texts*, p. 72.

²¹Bruno Meissner, *Babylonien und Assyrien* II, p. 119.

²²Cf. footnote 12.

²³Gustav Hölscher, *Hesekiel, Der Dichter und das Buch*, BZAW 39 (1924).

²⁴Cf. his proximity to sacral law, to which I have referred in my examinations of the peculiarities of prophetic speech in Ezekiel, ZAW 66 (1954), pp. 1–26. Reprinted in *Theologische Bücherei* 19 (1969), pp.

148–177. For all further details I must refer to my commentary on Ezekiel (see above, "Knowledge of God According to the Book of Ezekiel," footnote 100).

Plans for Rebuilding After the Catastrophe of 587

[1]Albrecht Alt, "Die Rolle Samarias bei der Entstehung des Judentums," in *Kleine Schriften zur Geschichte des Volkes Israel II* (1953), pp. 316–337.

[2]Gen. 2:7.

[3]Ezek. 37:1–14.

[4]Concerning the use of the name Israel in Ezekiel, cf. VT 8 (1958), pp. 75–90.

[5]Hos. 9:10; 13:5 f.; Jer. 2:1 ff.

[6]Ezek. 20; 23.

[7]Isa. 1:21.

[8]Ezek. 16. Concerning this, cf. my exposition in "History and Hermeneutic," *Journal for Theology and the Church* 4 (1967), pp. 1–13.

[9]Ezek. 2:5–8; 3:9, 26; 12:2 f., 9, 25; 17:12; 24:3; 44:6.

[10]G. Hölscher, *Hesekiel, der Dichter und das Buch*, BZAW 39 (1924).

[11]S. Herrmann, *Die prophetischen Heilserwartungen im Alten Testament*, BWANT 5, Folge, Heft 5 (1965).

[12]Ezekiel 36:17 ff. can show with particular clarity the extent to which the honor pledged to his people in his name motivates Yahweh to rescue his people. Cf., however, also 20:9, 14, 22, 44.

[13]Concerning this, cf. the exposition in ZAW 66 (1954), pp. 1–26; reprinted in Zimmerli, *Gottes Offenbarung*, ThB 19 (1963), pp. 148–77.

[14]Concerning all details I must refer to the exposition in my commentary on Ezekiel, *Ezekiel 1: A Commentary on the Book of the Prophet Ezekiel, Chapters 1—24*, trans. Ronald E. Clements (Philadelphia: Fortress, 1979), pp. 369–87; cf. also the German version (1955 ff.), pp. 794–809.

[15]Cf. A. Bertholet, *Der Verfassungsentwurf des Hesekiel in seiner religionsgeschichtlichen Bedeutung* (1922).

[16]For example, J. Wellhausen in his conclusions concerning the history of the priests and Levites in *Prolegomena to the History of Ancient Israel* (New York: Meridian Books, 1957), chapter 4, II, 2 ff.

[17]H. Gese, *Der Verfassungsentwurf des Ezechiel* (1957).

[18]40:3 reads: "whose appearance was like bronze"; cf. also the description of the creatures carrying the throne in 1:7.

[19]Cf. BK XIII, pp. 1192 f.

[20]Cf. the material in 28:11–19 or 31.

[21]40:5, in which the height of the surrounding wall is also given, is thus suspect as an addition.

[22]Temple- and *bnyn* -square.

[23]For example K. Galling in Fohrer-Galling, *Ezechiel*, HAT 13, pp. 225 f., who assumes a wall thickness of four cubits and thus an outer gate width of thirty-three cubits.

[24]Concerning the text, cf. Gese, *Der Verfassungsentwurf des Ezechiel*, pp. 39–41, footnote 4, and BK XIII, pp. 1072 f.

[25]Cf. M. Noth, *Könige*, BK IX (1964 ff.), pp. 95–167.

[26]In *Hebräische Wortforschung. Festschrift zum 80. Geburtstag von W. Baumgartner*, Suppl. VT 16 (1967), pp. 398–414; reprinted in Zimmerli, *Studien zur alttestamentlichen Theologie und Prophetie*, ThB 51 (1974), pp. 148–64.

[27]Cf. the plan G. A. Cooke offers at the conclusion of his commentary, *The Book of Ezekiel*, ICC (1936).

[28]Text in James B. Pritchard, *Ancient Near Eastern Texts*, 3rd ed. (Princeton, N.J.: Princeton University Press, 1969), pp. 106–109.

[29]Gen. 2:3.

[30]Inner dimension of the width and outer dimension of the length in 40:13, 15; cf. footnote 23.

[31]Figured from 40:48—41:4 and 41:5–13.

[32]40:47.

[33]41:13–15*a*.

[34]42:15–20.

[35]According to Lev. 25:9; cf. BK XIII, p. 995.

[36]1 Kings 7:2.

[37]If F. Maaß is correct in his conclusions concerning the fundamental passages of "Trito-Isaiah," then what has been said above is true in an even more direct sense, F. Maaß, "Tritojesaja?" in *Das ferne und nahe Wort. Festschrift für L. Rost*, BZAW 105 (1967), pp. 153–63.

[38]Cf. my observations in "Zur Sprache Tritojesajas," in *Festschrift für Ludwig Köhler* (1950), pp. 62–74; reprinted in *Gottes Offenbarung* (1969), pp. 217–233.

[39]Cf. a more thorough discussion in Zimmerli, "Das Gnadenjahr des Herrn," in *Studien zur alttestamentlichen Theologie und Prophetie*, pp. 222–34.

[40]Concerning the text, cf. BK XIII, p. 1072.

[41]Amos 7:13.

[42]Cf. further Jer. 26 and 36.

[43]Cf., for example, the description in H. Bonnet, *Reallexikon der ägyptischen Religionsgeschichte* (1952), p. 798: "It (the temple) stands . . . in a . . . fortress-like walled enclosure and is also surrounded by tile structures, living and work rooms that open up like a palace to the first of the two antecourts . . . Ramses III, like his predecessor Ramses II, had a chapel off the first large columned hall."

⁴⁴According to this theory, only the king is the true priest in Egypt: "Only the God-King is permitted to approach the god in the temple on equal footing," H. Kees, *Das Priestertum im ägyptischen Staat vom Neuen Reich bis zur Spätzeit* (1953), p. 1.

⁴⁵D. Neiman, "PGR: A Canaanite Cult-Object in the Old Testament," JBL 67 (1948), pp. 55–60; K. Galling, "Erwägungen zum Stelenheiligtum von Hazor," ZDPV 75 (1959), pp. 1–13.

⁴⁶From this perspective one can correct the sketches of the temple layout in Cooke (cf. footnote 27), Bertholet-Galling (*Hesekiel*, HAT 13 [1936], p. 141), and even in Walther Eichrodt's *Ezekiel: A Commentary*, trans. Cosslett Quin (London: SCM Press, 1970), p. 537.

⁴⁷41:13, *bnyh*.

⁴⁸1 Chronicles 26:16 appears to speak quite naturally about a west gate in the temple area; in view of the expansion of the municipal area beyond the Tyropoeon Valley, such a gate would be extremely likely. Cf. further J. Simons, *Jerusalem in the Old Testament* (1952), pp. 426 and 428.

⁴⁹E. Würthwein, *Der 'amm ha' arez im Alten Testament*, BWANT 4, Folge, Heft 17 (1936), especially pp. 47–50.

⁵⁰E. Unger, *Babylon, die heilige Stadt nach der Beschreibung der Babylonier* (1931), especially chapter 19, "Die Heilige Pforte," pp. 201–206. Cf. also A. Pohl, "Das verschlossene Tor, Ez. 44:1–3," Bibl 13 (1932), pp. 90–92 and others.

⁵¹B. Landsberger, *Der kultische Kalender der Babylonier und Assyrer*, Leipziger semitistische Studien 6 (1915), p. 87.

⁵²One should probably also understand Psalm 99:5 in this context.

⁵³2 Kings 18:4. Cf. also Zimmerli, "Das Bilderverbot in der Geschichte des alten Israel. Goldenes Kalb, eherne Schlange, Mazzeben und Lade," in *Studien zur alttestamentlichen Theologie und Prophetie*, pp. 247–260.

⁵⁴The clear parallel relationship between ark and throne in this passage appears to me (in addition to other observations) to controvert the attempt of J. Maier, *Das altisraelitische Ladeheiligtum*, BZAW 93, (1965) to deny that the ark has the character of a throne and to refer such character only to the cherub placed above the ark.

⁵⁵According to Psalm 132:8, the topos "place of my rest" (*mqwm mnwhty*) also belongs to the "word universe" of "ark theology."

⁵⁶Concerning what follows, cf. also O. Procksch, "Fürst und Priester bei Hesekiel," ZAW 58 (1940/41), pp. 99–133, and concerning the distinction between *mlk* and *nśy'* especially p. 116.

⁵⁷1 Sam. 8; 10:17–27; 12; and Hos. 7:3; 8:4.

⁵⁸The insertion of 44:4 ff., which we will discuss later, disrupts the connection between 44:3 and the regulations for the *nśy'* in 45 and 46. Further editorial additions in 45 make it difficult to determine the exact connecting point in 45. Cf. the commentary.

[59]The new employment of the vestibule again clearly discloses that this gate is perpetually closed.

[60]Concerning the designation of this congregation as 'm h'rṣ, cf. footnote 49.

[61]In any case, both the Melchizedek tradition in Psalm 110 and the list of officials in 2 Samuel 8:18 still show us something of the priestly function of the king (and his sons).

[62]If indeed this is a messianic statement—something S. Herrmann contests, Die prophetischen Heilserwartungen im Alten Testament, p. 258.

[63]This is particularly true in the case of the exiles, in whose situation the radical organization of property relationships within the country is particularly easy to understand. This "point zero" is not a factor in the same way for those who stayed in the land.

[64]Num. 32; Josh. 13.

[65]Concerning the discussion of the northern boundary, cf. BK XIII, pp. 1213–16.

[66]This is how it is formulated in 47:14; cf. also 20:6.

[67]After the elimination of the landless Levi, the number twelve is attained by splitting Joseph into the partial tribes Manasseh and Ephraim, something noted in the gloss 47:13b. Concerning the numbering of the tribes, cf. M. Noth, Das System des zwölf Stämme Israels, BWANT 4. Folge, Heft 1 (1930).

[68]C. M. Mackay's thesis that the sanctuary lies somewhere in the vicinity of Shechem, a thesis he has defended in various essays (cf. BK XIII, p. 1202), cannot be supported.

[69]Cf. Exod. 25:2 f. or Num. 18:26–29 and elsewhere.

[70]The predominance of the number 25 extends to this plan as well.

[71]48:10, 18, 20 f. (45:6 f.).

[72]This was probably located on the south side of the square.

[73]Jerusalem only appears under the designation "the city." This emphasizes with particular clarity its special position among the majority of Israel's cities, a position this plan does not really deny.

[74]M. Noth, "Das Krongut der israelitischen Könige und seine Versaltung," ZDPV 50 (1927), pp. 211–44. What has been shown to be the case here for the northern Israelite kings was probably also basically true in the Southern Kingdom. Ezekiel 48 is thinking in terms of the overall Israelite state of affairs.

[75]In the postexilic regulations we find nothing of this trwmh-regulation for priests and Levites and certainly not for the line of David. It was not able to assert itself.

[76]Cf. "Der Wahrheitserweis Jahwes nach der Botschaft der beiden Exilspropheten," in Zimmerli, Studien zur alttestamentlichen Theologie und Prophetie, pp. 192–212.

[77]44:10, 15 (then in the addition 48:11).

[78]We also need to mention here Ezekiel 15 with its terrifying assertion of Israel's almost inherent uselessness.

[79]44:15, then also the supplement 40:46*b* (Gese, *Der Verfassungsentwurf des Ezechiel*, p. 22, footnote 1).

[80]A. H. J. Gunneweg, *Leviten und Priester*, FRLANT 89 (1965).

[81]2 Kings 23:8.

[82]Cf. also 18:6, 11, 15.

[83]For example, Ezra 8:15. The lists in Ezra 2 and Nehemiah 7, however, with their quotas for priests and Levites, also speak a clear language.

[84]According to Numbers 3:11–13, the service of the Levites is consecrated as a representative for the first-born of Israel in service at the sanctuary. Concerning this, cf. "Erstgeborene und Leviten. Ein Beitrag zur exilisch-nachexilischen Theologie," in Zimmerli, *Studien zur alttestamentlichen Theologie und Prophetie*, pp. 235–46.

[85]Gunneweg, *Leviten und Priester*, p. 33 concerning Exod. 32:29 and passim.

[86]Cf. F. Horst, "Zwei Begriffe für Eigentum (Besitz): *nḥlh* und *'ḥzh*, in *Verbannung und Heimkehr. Festschrift für W. Rudolph* (1961), pp. 135–56.

[87]Here in 41:4 the "most holy" (*qdš hqdšym*) is only the *cella* of the temple.

[88]44:15 f.

[89]The later textual gloss *mngb* in 40:2 would like to produce this kind of relationship.

[90]Does the *yhwh šmh* intend a distant allusion to *yrwšlm*?

[91]The name Zion occurs nowhere in the entire book of Ezekiel.

[92]Cf. BK XIII, p. 1093.

[93]We could also mention here the Zion Psalms 46; 48; and 76.